YEAH! YEAH! YEAH!

WITHDRAWN

The Beatles, Beatlemania, and the Music That Changed the World

BY **BOB SPITZ**

LITTLE, BROWN AND COMPANY

New York ❦ Boston

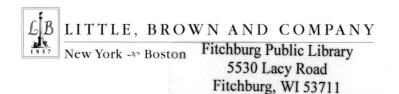

Fitchburg Public Library
5530 Lacy Road
Fitchburg, WI 53711

PHOTO CREDITS
© Getty Images / Hulton Archive, p. i. © Mirrorpix, pp. viii, 14, 32, 52, 60–61, 72, 88, 112, 134, 154, 170, 188, and 206.
© Corbis, p. 221.

Little, Brown and Company

Hachette Book Group USA
237 Park Avenue, New York, NY 10017
Visit our Web site at www.lb-kids.com

First Edition: October 2007

Some material in this book is adapted from *The Beatles: The Biography* by Bob Spitz.

Library of Congress Cataloging-in-Publication Data

Spitz, Bob.
  Yeah! yeah! yeah! : the Beatles, Beatlemania, and the music that changed the world / by Bob Spitz.—1st ed.
    p. cm.
  Summary: The *New York Times* bestselling biography of the Beatles, in a style and format for young readers.
  ISBN-13: 978-0-316-11555-1
  ISBN-10: 0-316-11555-X
  1. Beatles—Juvenile literature. 2. Rock musicians—England—Biography—Juvenile literature. I. Spitz, Bob. Beatles. II. Title.
  ML3930.B39S65 2007
  782.42166092'2—dc22   2006039575
  [B]

10 9 8 7 6 5 4 3 2 1

WOR

Printed in the United States of America

Book design by Alison Impey

The text was set in Esprit and Caecilia, and the display type is Akzidenz Grotesk.

For Lily and Her Posse:
Sylvia, Sarah & Lineth

CONTENTS

Chapter 1

AN INCREDIBLE DISCOVERY

"Miracles are for dreamers," John Lennon once complained to a friend. Of course, this was long after an extraordinary event transformed him into a world-famous figure—and following a night when his dreams were most likely as vivid as an action-adventure movie.

As miracles go, this one would last a lifetime.

It occurred when John was sixteen, on a blistering hot Saturday afternoon, July 6, 1957, in a place that catered to divine intervention: St. Peter's Church in Woolton, a village on the outskirts of Liverpool, England. John and his friends waited all year for the church's annual garden festival, which was the biggest social event on the village calendar. It seemed as if the entire community turned out to mingle, listen to music, and await the crowning of the Rose Queen at the conclusion of the day's festivities. There was something for everyone to enjoy, plenty of attractions to dazzle the eyes. Dozens of stalls covered the grounds that separated the sanctuary from the old church hall and spilled over onto two surrounding fields like a carnival midway. Long tables were set up on the grass, covered with sandwiches, cakes, and lacquered candy apples. Used books were stacked for sale, and racks of clothing attracted bargain hunters. Lemonade stands were posted across from wooden booths where children played ringtoss, darts, horseshoes, and other games to win fabulous prizes.

For John, the festival was an all-out blast. No day ever took so long to arrive, passed so quickly, or seemed as magical. But this year, a special thrill raised his anticipation.

In the past, only military bands had been invited to entertain at the festival. The crowds that lined the church field would cheer as men in stiff blue uniforms played marches and other patriotic music to pump up the excitement. But a crucial change had been taking place that affected what would be heard this year. Kids had begun listening to new types of music, including rock 'n roll and something called skiffle, a kind of souped-up folk music that had started a craze among British teenagers. Skiffle caught on because it was so easy to play; all anyone needed to form a skiffle group was a guitar or a banjo, a rippled washboard, and a homemade bass, made by poking a broom handle through an upturned metal

What Is Skiffle?

Before rock 'n roll caught fire in the Liverpool clubs, jazz ruled. During intermissions, however, some of the musicians cobbled together a confection of sounds to fill the gap. They'd play homemade instruments like a "tea chest" bass, which was an old washtub with a strange broomstick-and-rope attachment, accompanied by a washboard and perhaps a guitar. Called skiffle, the music was an odd assortment of American blues, spirituals, and folk songs like "Rock Island Line" and "Pick a Bale of Cotton."

Skiffle group the Rebels, circa 1956.
© TERRY CRYER/CORBIS

It was the offhand charm of skiffle that captured Great Britain's imagination. Rock 'n roll was too much, too fast; skiffle was a compromise. "It was music we could play right away and sound okay doing right away," said the Quarry Men's Eric Griffiths. And it enthralled Liverpool audiences, not because it was new but because it was so unexpectedly familiar. It wasn't long before most of the 328 clubs in Liverpool were involved in some sort of skiffle show. And its greatest fan was a fifteen-year-old boy named John Lennon.

bucket and attaching a cord to pluck. The sound they made was unimportant. Skiffle was all about having fun.

John and a few friends from the neighborhood had started their own skiffle group called the Quarry Men, after Quarry Bank High School, which they attended. It wasn't really much of a band, nor was John much of a musician. He only knew a few chords on the guitar, which "he beat the daylights out of," according to a friend. And the band itself just made sort of "a general noise." But that did not seem to matter. The Quarry Men *looked* professional. They put up posters all over town and played at parties and local talent contests where you weren't judged as much on ability as you were on spirit.

As it happened, one of the boys' mothers convinced the church festival committee that a skiffle band would give this year's gala an extra shot of excitement, and she proposed the Quarry Men—most of whom, she assured the committee members, had been confirmed at St. Peter's—as the obvious choice.

The boys were understandably ecstatic. "It wasn't simply the honor of playing there that excited us," recalled Nigel Walley, who functioned as the group's manager. "Everyone's parents and grandparents would be there, as would all our friends." So there was every opportunity for them to make a powerful impression.

John was especially restless. As the leader, he thought of the Quarry Men as *his* band, and he was eager for them to put on a good show. Besides, he knew that his mother and aunt would be among the crowd, and it would be their first chance to see him perform.

The Quarry Men weren't scheduled to play until four o'clock. In the meantime, the boys drifted around the grounds and stopped to watch a Liverpool police dog obedience display, featuring Alsatians trained to jump through flaming hoops. The Band of the Cheshire Yeomanry—an outfit comparable to the US National Guard—was on the uncovered stage, warming up the crowd. It wasn't long before they were replaced by the Quarry Men, who played a spirited set of songs—half skiffle, half rock 'n roll—that was greeted enthusiastically by the teenagers pressed around the stage.

John recalled, "It was the first day I did 'Be-Bop-A-Lula' live on stage," and one can

only imagine how he rocked out. The singing was no doubt loud and raunchy, the sound only slightly better than awful. John could never remember the words to songs, preferring to make up his own, which were often hilarious, as he went along. Sometimes he stumbled over words or just grunted, it made no difference to him, but today his improvisation was fairly sharp and witty. He spotted his aunt Mimi standing in the crowd and inserted a few clever lines about her on the spot, to everyone's delight.

Shortly before the Quarry Men were finished, they noticed a mate named Ivan Vaughan standing below them, off to the right of the stage, with another boy at his side. Smiles were exchanged, and somehow it was understood that they would all hook up after the show.

Afterward, Ivan charged backstage to congratulate the Quarry Men on their performance. He said hello to everyone, then introduced his friend—Paul McCartney.

"I think you two will get along," he said to John, perhaps the understatement of all time.

Paul was only fifteen but looked even younger, with a round, pudgy face, a tight little rosebud mouth, and droopy eyes like a spaniel's. This isn't to imply that he was an odd-looking boy. There was a handsome quality that came through in his features, as well as something strong and instinctive. Even as a teenager, Paul was rather clever about people, sizing them up and fitting in. It was clear that he was comfortable around older boys; nevertheless, John expected him to show a little respect, especially in the presence of such celebrated musicians. But Paul wasn't intimidated; he came on like gangbusters.

The Quarry Men perform at the Woolton church fete, July 6, 1957. The photo was taken fifteen minutes before John Lennon was introduced to Paul McCartney. From left to right: Eric Griffiths, Rod Davis, John, Pete Shotton, Len Garry. © LONDON FEATURES INTERNATIONAL

Paul's class at Liverpool Institute, circa 1955. © Mirrorpix

Instead of hanging back and observing, he picked up his guitar. "Mind if I play?" he asked, as they sat around on the backstage benches. Without waiting for a reply, he launched into "Whole Lotta Shakin' Goin' On," a rock 'n roll hit that the Quarry Men had been unable to learn. Then, Paul recalled, "I did 'Twenty Flight Rock' *and* knew all the words." In fact, he did more than just play the song, he *performed* it, cutting loose on the vocals, howling the lyrics with a little catch in his throat that made him sound like Elvis Presley. He wasn't too shabby on the guitar, either. Nigel Walley remembered, "He played with a cool, authoritative touch." There was a tricky little chord change that none of them had been able to figure out, and Paul handled it effortlessly, vamping on the guitar strings with the heel of his hand.

John saw right off that the boy had talent, not to mention plenty of nerve. He came on so loose and confident, without any inhibitions; there didn't seem to be a self-conscious bone in his body. John couldn't take his eyes off him. "I was very impressed by Paul playing 'Twenty Flight Rock,'" he admitted. "He could obviously play the guitar. I half thought to myself, 'He's as good as me.'"

In fact, he was better—much better. Paul was a gifted singer and an accomplished musician, while John could barely scratch out three measly chords. Plus, Paul had all the right moves. "It was uncanny," recalled Eric Griffiths, another member of the Quarry Men. "He could play and sing in a way that none of us could, including John. It was so natural. We couldn't get enough of it. It was a real eye-opener."

Afterward, a friend remembered, "John and Paul circled each other like cats." Their interest in each other was deep, complicated, and strong—a magnetic pull. There was something they recognized in each other, but it also repelled them, perhaps because it struck too close to home. Neither boy knew exactly what it was, but they could feel it. Instead of becoming instant friends, they played it cool, acting polite toward each other, interested but not *too* interested.

Later that night, walking home with his friend Pete Shotton, John appeared to be lost in thought. He didn't seem interested in talking about the fun they'd had at the festival or even about the Quarry Men's well-received performance. At first, Pete suspected that something was wrong, but he shrugged it off as one of John's moods. Besides, Pete knew not to press his friend. It was a beautiful night, and they walked without talking most of the way. Finally, John broke the silence. "What did you think of that kid, Paul?" he asked Pete.

So *that* was it, Pete thought. All this time, he had been worried that something serious was up, when John was simply preoccupied with that new boy on the scene, Paul—Paul McCartney. Pete was instantly jealous. He and John were best friends, best mates, and now he sensed someone else creeping onto their turf. Two's company, three's a crowd, Pete thought. But he knew how important music was to his friend, so he put his jealousy aside and answered truthfully. "I liked him, actually," he said. "I thought he was really good."

John nodded and walked on in silence. He was haunted by Paul McCartney's display of skill, the way he had handled the guitar so smoothly and with such panache, the way he'd sung all the correct words to the rock 'n roll songs. All of that led to a more important issue. He was thinking about asking Paul to join the band, but there were some built-in headaches that troubled him. "I'd been the kingpin up to then," John remembered thinking. "Now I thought, if I take him on, what will happen? He was good, so he was worth having." And John thought Paul looked a little like Elvis. "I dug him." Still, the Quarry Men was *his* band; *he* was the rightful leader. All the other guys looked up to him. If he let Paul join, he knew they'd have to be equals, and he hated giving up any control of the group. He also feared being shown up by Paul, that Paul would expose his shortcomings as a musician.

John remembered turning over many questions in his head that night. "Was it better to have a guy who was better than the [others]? To make the group stronger, or to let me be stronger?" Then again, would he really lose anything by inviting Paul to play with the band? Could Paul's incredible talent possibly rub off on him, make him that much better?

Even with all this uncertainty, the decision had already been made. Hearing Paul play and sing that night had really knocked John out. That had sealed it, as far as he was concerned. He couldn't believe a guy who was relatively close to him in age and living only a short distance away could have so much to offer. What an incredible discovery! There was also something unique about Paul, something John couldn't quite put his finger on, that intensified his interest. Hooking up with someone like that was too exciting to pass up. John sensed he was on the verge of something important. Sure, they could make some music together and have a little fun, but there was something else, something indescribable that intrigued him. Whatever it was would become apparent in time.

Little did he know it would turn into the Beatles.

· · · · ·

Miracles, such as they are, occur at the most unexpected times—and in the most unusual places. That John Lennon and Paul McCartney met at all is an amazing phenomenon; that it happened in Liverpool, England, of all places, is even more remarkable.

Until the end of World War II, Liverpool was one of the most diverse and thriving cities in Europe. With its strategic location on a crescent at the mouth of the Mersey River where it meets the Irish Sea, Liverpool functioned as "the Gateway to the British Empire," if not to the rest of the world. Water played a key role in Liverpool's early supremacy. Most of the early twentieth century's greatest sailing vessels, including the *Titanic* and the *Queen Mary,* were constructed by its master artisans, turning Liverpool into a shipbuilding center that catered to international trade. Not a day seemed to pass when fleets of tall-masted ships and steamers weren't on the move in and out of the port, bound for one of the globe's imagined corners. With its bustling docks and jungle of warehouses bulging cargo, Liverpool attracted sailors, traders, craftsmen, merchants, and dreamers of big dreams, people seeking their fortunes in a city loaded with opportunity.

"In the early days," George Harrison recalled, "Liverpool was really busy." But during World War II, the city suffered terribly at the hands of the relentless German bombers. Every night, planes strafed the unprotected port, setting the docks on fire and causing severe damage to the surrounding area. "They were sinking millions of tons of shipping," according to a local scholar who lived through the attacks. "We couldn't feed ourselves, couldn't restock our army." Entire neighborhoods were destroyed in the air strikes that pounded the city. Ringo Starr remembered seeing "big gaps in the street where houses had stood." Liverpool survived, thanks in large part to the American forces stationed nearby, but the city never recovered.

From that time on, Liverpool slid into a long and steady decline. Most of the shipping business moved south, closer to London, while Liverpool

Liverpool family left homeless from bombing. © Hulton-Deutsch Collection/CORBIS

struggled to keep its head held high. "It was going poor, a very poor city, and tough," John remembered. "But people [there] have a great sense of humor; they are always cracking jokes." A tireless sense of humor was the way they kept their spirits up during times of great hardship. Strange as it may seem, almost everyone in Liverpool thought of himself as a comedian. In fact, many of England's most famous comics grew up there, where being funny seemed to come naturally.

"Liverpool has its own identity," said Paul, who always felt a distinct difference living there. "It's even got its own accent," called scouse, a sleepy, singsongy drawl that made everything sound like a punch line. The word itself comes from a nautical term for a sailors' stew consisting of leftovers, and in a way, scouse is a little bit of many regional accents mixed together and steeped in the sea. To John, however, it sounded flat and strangled. "We talk through our noses," he said, none too complimentary. But there was something rhythmic to it, something almost musical, which should come as no surprise considering what eventually developed.

In fact, music played a prominent part in Liverpool's cultural identity. The city owed its fascinating character in part to a long and rich tradition of song, the legacy of a broad spectrum of immigrants who arrived in its port. In the early 1800s, "stout little ships" brought slaves from Africa and the West Indies, and with them came exotic melodies and rhythms that streamed into the cultural pipeline. Later in the century, nearly fifty thousand Irish refugees poured into Liverpool, adding their own music to the mix, so that the blend was multiracial and international.

Throughout the twentieth century, Liverpool was alive with music. The city boasted more than twenty fabulous music halls, which packed in crowds every night of the week, two shows a night. All the factories sponsored brass bands that gave weekly concerts in the parks. Dances were staged in a variety of ballrooms that featured live swing bands. People routinely sang in the pubs. "You could walk down any street, any time of the day," recalled a Liverpudlian, "and hear music coming out of practically every window."

After the war, a new wave of music came through the port. "It's where the sailors

Hank Williams. © MICHAEL OCHS ARCHIVES/REDFERNS

Woody Guthrie. © MICHAEL OCHS ARCHIVES/ REDFERNS

Leadbelly. © MICHAEL OCHS ARCHIVES/REDFERNS

would come home on the ships, with…records from America," John Lennon recalled. Initially, country music caught on quickly in the local clubs. "I heard country-and-western music in Liverpool before I heard rock 'n roll." George Harrison's father, who served as a merchant seaman, brought home records by Jimmy Rogers and Slim Whitman, two legendary American country music artists. Ringo remembered: "A lot of it was around from the guys in the navy. I'd go to parties, and they'd be putting on [records by] Hank Williams, Hank Snow, and all those country acts." There was a time, right after the war, when Liverpool was regarded as "the Nashville of the North" for its rich deposit of country attractions performing the latest twangy rave as soon as another ship anchored in port.

But the American musical influence wasn't limited to country. "We were hearing old funky blues records in Liverpool that people across Britain or Europe had never heard about or knew about, only in the port areas," said John.

George gravitated to music by Big Bill Broonzy, Leadbelly, and Woody Guthrie, which he said was "more like rural blues and bluegrass, not rock 'n roll." That would come later. Paul, who was also a musically curious lad, followed the same general direction. "There were records other than rock 'n roll that were important to me," Paul said. His older cousin Bett had what he called "a fairly grown-up record collection" that kept him fascinated as

11

a kid. "Bett would play me records like Peggy Lee's 'Fever.' Peggy Lee did 'Till There Was You' [one of the Beatles' early numbers], as well. This led me to songs like 'A Taste of Honey' and things which were slightly to the left and right of rock 'n roll."

As young boys, the future Beatles listened to different types of music that would ultimately affect and shape their sound. "John's, George's, and my tastes were all pretty much in common," Paul explained. "We shared our influences like mad. And when John would show another side to his musical taste, it would be similar to what I'd been brought up on, like my dad's music."

Paul's father, Jim McCartney, played trumpet in a jazz band, as well as the piano, on which he taught his son the basic chord changes and time signatures. "He had a lot of music in him," Paul recalled. "Whenever John sang, I automatically sang in harmony with him, and that's due to my dad's teaching. I was very influenced by him." Ringo's mother, Elsie, played the piano, John's mother played the ukulele, and George's father learned the guitar while he was at sea.

Circa 1955: still life of a Bendix brand radio sitting on a table. © James G. Welgos/Welgos/Getty Images

There was music in all of their houses, just as there was music everywhere in Liverpool. "You couldn't avoid it," recalled John's friend Pete Shotton. It was part of the atmosphere. The neighborhood boys delighted in singing together in the park. In the summer, they'd recline on the grass against their overturned bikes, wait for someone to cut them on the harmonica, then throw their heads back and sing: "Keep a-movin', Dan, don't you listen to him, Dan, he's a devil not a man…" Or: "I'm just a-walkin' in the rain…" The boys had plenty of material to work from, thanks to well-stocked jukeboxes at Hilda's Chip Shop and the Dutch

Café, where they discovered records by Johnnie Ray, Frankie Laine, and Tennessee Ernie Ford. "We thought they were great because of all the expression in their voices," Pete recalled. "Especially Frankie Laine, who was putting a lot of feeling into everything [he sang]."

It was the feeling, in particular, that eventually turned the tide.

John Lennon, Paul McCartney, George Harrison, and Ringo Starr shared a love of popular music, but the feeling, such as it was, belonged to a generation that looked and acted more like their parents. There was precious little in those hammy ballads that actually spoke to teenagers. Oh, they *liked* the moods and melodies, but there was little, if anything, that genuinely excited them. The music didn't *speak* to them in a way that expressed teenagers' feelings, the insecurity and anxieties they were struggling with. Johnnie Ray, Frankie Laine, and Tennessee Ernie Ford were cool and suave as singers go, but they weren't any teenager's idea of role models—or heroes.

Then, one weekend night in 1956, teenagers in Liverpool began picking up a radio signal from faraway Luxembourg. It crackled with static and faded in and out according to the ever-changing weather over the Irish Sea. But it was enough to hold young listeners captive, straining to hear every syllable coming over the airwaves.

For a while, no one knew what to make of the music they heard over Radio Luxembourg or what it was called, only that it "was absolutely wonderful and very exotic." Sometime later an announcer finally put a name to it. He called it rock 'n roll, and it would forever change their lives.

Chapter 2

Rock 'n roll!

"That's the music that brought me from the provinces of England to the world," John Lennon recalled later, after he helped to transform its sound and shape a generation. "That's what made me what I am."

To teenagers everywhere in the late 1950s, rock 'n roll was the rallying cry, the raw, combustible sound that connected them to one another, defined their adolescence, and provided a voice with which they could express themselves. The music touched on everything teenagers were grappling with: angst, impatience, love, sexuality, insecurity, rebellion, and fantasy—all hooked up to a powerful suggestive beat. The name alone captured the future Beatles' imaginations. *Rock 'n roll* suggested thrills, something loud and disruptive, a certain disobedience in the way they could dance to it and what it said. The excitement of the music broke through all the boundaries, carrying listeners to places unknown. "When I hear good rock," John said, "I just fall apart and I have no other interest in life. The world could be ending if rock 'n roll is playing."

Astonishingly, the first stirrings of rock 'n roll had escaped John Lennon's ears. "In our family, the radio was hardly ever on, so I got to [it] later," he recalled. "Not like Paul and George." There was a steely decorum in the house where John grew up, an almost religious code of discipline implemented by his aunt Mimi Smith, who was a stern, no-nonsense woman. If anyone presumed that Mimi would sanction rock 'n roll, they had a rude awakening coming.

John, May 1948, a few weeks after he entered Dovedale Primary School in Allerton. © Tom Hanley/Camera Press (Text & Illustrations) London

Even though Mimi was tough on John, he adored his aunt with a mixture of admiration and awe. She could be a "merciless disciplinarian," according to those who knew her, but she was also an easy touch with a big heart. It was Mimi who raised John, stressed the absolute necessity for self-education, and instilled in him a lifelong love of words. Her husband, George, a kind, gentle soul, taught John to read "syllable by syllable" at the age of four, after which he promptly blazed through the fantastic stories in *Alice's Adventures in Wonderland*, *The Wind in the Willows*, and the Just William series. "He had such an imagination and built up the stories himself when he and I talked them over," Mimi recalled. George recited John's favorite nursery rhymes and, when he was old enough, taught John how to solve crossword puzzles. "Words needn't have to be taken at their face value," he explained. "They had many meanings"—valuable advice saved for later. Aunt Mimi and Uncle George tirelessly devoted themselves to John's happiness, but despite their goodwill, he never stopped thinking about his parents.

Occasionally, John told friends that he was an orphan, most likely as a defense against his lingering unhappiness. But in truth, his parents had abandoned him by the time he was six. His mother, Julia, a headstrong free spirit, was an outgoing and vivacious woman who craved distractions, laughs, and excitement. The youngest of five sisters, she was blessed with a wicked sense of humor, as well as a fanciful way of looking at life. Night after night, humming with energy, she made the rounds of local dance halls, where she found herself in great demand as a partner in the stylish jitterbug competitions that lasted into the early hours of morning. She could tell a joke as hard and spicy as any man, which won her no shortage of admirers. And, according to one of John's cousins, she sang—"with a voice like Vera Lynn," it was said—at the drop of a hat.

Julia was twenty when she met Freddie Lennon, John's father. He'd been raised in a prestigious Liverpool orphanage, where he earned a reputation for being happy-go-lucky. "Anywhere Freddie turned up always meant fun was about to start," recalled a relative. "He couldn't resist having a good time." Like Julia, there wasn't a room he couldn't light up with a hilarious remark or his screwball character. Wittiness came easily to Freddie, and he carried it off with such vitality that friends assumed he would capitalize on his personality. But he was never able to put it all together.

From the moment Freddie and Julia met, they were inseparable. They entertained each other, made each other laugh in ways that complemented their fancy-free spirits. Both tireless dreamers, they spent long days walking around Liverpool, hatching schemes. Perhaps they would open a shop, a pub, a café, or a club where they would take turns performing, Julia cracking one-liners, Freddie singing and playing the banjo. He had a pretty good voice, a husky tenor, and no shortage of charisma. But despite all the vaudeville theaters in the city, there was no steady work and very little money. Too frivolous to master a vocation, Freddie bounced from office job to odd job, borrowing money from friends and an older brother.

Finally Freddie escaped this dilemma by the route chosen most often by Liverpool men: he put to sea. He signed on to a ship headed toward the Mediterranean, working as a merchant navy steward and later as a headwaiter. Onboard a succession of ocean liners, traveling between the Greek islands, North Africa, and the West Indies, Freddie became a crew favorite because of his personable nature. Passengers remembered seeing him weave among tables "with a smile that sparkled in a room." But the job meant that he was away from home most of the year. Even when John was born, on October 9, 1940, Freddie was gone, having shipped out on a troop transport earlier that month, doing his part for the war effort.

For the first few years of John's life, Julia threw herself into motherhood, devoting all her efforts to raising her son. Freddie reappeared every now and again, but it was only for a day or two, and then he was off once more on some woolly seaborne adventure.

An easy childhood for John was never in the cards. Julia wasn't cut out for motherhood. With John demanding more attention, balancing her obligations became too much for Julia. She did what she could, but with her husband gone and a young son to take care of, there was only so much she could handle. What's more, Julia longed to spin back into the vibrant social scene. Any sensitive child would pick up the signals, and John, who was uniquely perceptive, interpreted his mother's frustrations as being his fault. Reminiscences about his childhood were always filled with guilt. It was the rejection he remembered most, the feeling that he was in the way, the source of Julia's unhappiness and Freddie's absence.

"The worst pain is that of not being wanted," John admitted, "of realizing your parents do not need you in the way you need them." Throughout his life, John Lennon grappled with the feeling that he "was never really wanted." Life became harder still when Julia and Freddie decided to separate. John found himself embroiled in a series of melodramas, each one more traumatic and gut-wrenching than the last.

Freddie put out to sea again, leaving no information as to his whereabouts. He remained just a vague shadow figure in John's life and, except for two brief appearances, had no direct influence on his son's upbringing. Julia moved in with another man, one whose temper could erupt without warning. "He had a very short fuse," recalled one of John's cousins. Julia knew when to get out of his way, but occasionally there was violence. This and other neglect took an early toll on John. "It confused him, and he often ran away," Mimi told an interviewer, recalling the times she opened the door to find her nephew cowering in tears, unable to speak. More than once, Mimi took John back to Julia's, where she gave her younger sister a piece of her mind. Julia tried to organize a model of family life in her new situation, but within weeks John was no longer living with her.

The exact circumstances surrounding this development have been blurred by myth. There may have been some friction between Julia and the new man in her life; perhaps the presence of a young boy put too much strain on their relationship. Some relatives have suggested that Julia simply wasn't up to the responsibility of full-time motherhood. None of this made any difference to John. He seemed to believe that it was somehow his fault, that he was to blame for Julia's incompetence. "My mother...couldn't cope with me" was the way he later explained it. Whatever the reason, at some point John was sent outright to Mimi's, once and for all, where it was determined he would receive "a proper upbringing."

Ten-year-old John Lennon in 1951, standing outside Mendips, his aunt Mimi's home in Woolton. © Tom Hanley/Camera Press (Text & Illustrations) London

19

In almost no time, John settled comfortably into the Smith household. The family residence on Menlove Avenue—nicknamed Mendips, after an English mountain range—was as familiar as any he'd ever known, a cozy seven-room stucco-and-brick cottage. Sunlight filled the pleasant interior, warming an endless warren of nooks where John often curled up and paged dreamily through picture books. His bedroom was a small but peaceful alcove over the porch, from where he could smell the sweet apple tarts and crumbles Mimi baked almost as effortlessly as John later wrote songs. Aunt Mimi and Uncle George made John feel loved there. Besides, Julia visited often, practically every day, which in some ways made the arrangement better for John, and in other ways made it worse.

John's childhood may have been confusing and painful, but unlike the loner persona he cultivated later on, he wasn't an outcast. Contrary to later public opinion, he wasn't lonesome or isolated. Nor was he "very deprived" as a child, as others sometimes claimed. "I was well protected by my auntie and uncle, and they looked after me very well," John insisted.

Instead, the questions he grappled with growing up were why he felt *different,* and how he could cultivate the ideas churning inside him. And what, if anything, would open up the world for a well-adjusted but bored middle-class kid from suburban Liverpool? He found the answer quite by chance one night in the privacy of his bedroom, as he was scanning the radio dial.

• • • • •

Thanks to geography and the cosmos, Radio Luxembourg had a signal that by some miracle found its way from its origin, tucked between Brussels, Germany, and France, all the way to Liverpool. Everything depended on the weather masses that collided over the Irish Sea. "There was always a bad reception—you'd have [to put] your ear to the speaker, always fiddling with the dial," recalls one of Paul McCartney's classmates, "but it would give you plenty to dream about."

Elvis Presley performing onstage. © Michael Ochs Archives/Redferns

Every Saturday and Sunday night in the late 1950s, three of the boys who would later become the Beatles (George, the youngest, was asleep by airtime) sat in their darkened bedrooms, tuning in to the station's staticky signal as Radio Luxembourg's deejays introduced the rock 'n roll records that were climbing the American charts. They were mesmerized by the music's big, aggressive beat and the tidal spill of lyrics. The effect it had on them was awesome. Sometimes the boys would furiously jot down lyrics to the songs; other times, overcome by a thrilling piece of music, they would push their tablets away, lean back, close their eyes, and let themselves be carried off by the voices and the melodies that would have a lasting influence on their lives.

They loved the blues and rockabilly tunes that blared through their speakers. Early rock 'n roll pioneers like Bill Haley, Carl Perkins, and Chuck Berry genuinely excited them. But it was Elvis Presley who really captured their imaginations. In the spring of 1956, with the debut of Presley's "Heartbreak Hotel," an explosion was felt by teenage listeners unlike anything that had ever hit them before. "When I heard it," John recalled, "it was the end for me. Nothing really affected me until Elvis." His friend Pete Shotton agreed, especially about "Heartbreak Hotel," saying, "It was the most exciting thing [we'd] ever heard."

Paul with his father, Jim McCartney. © MIRRORPIX

Paul's discovery of Elvis was even more rapturous. "That was him," Paul said, "that was the guru we'd been waiting for. The messiah had arrived."

From the age of fourteen, Paul learned to copy Elvis's style and sound, capturing the familiar twang as well as the hiccup in his voice. "He was an incredible vocalist," Paul said. "Elvis made a huge impression on me."

And Paul in turn made a huge impression on John, first at the garden fete and later in the months that followed. More than his ability or his singing voice, both of which were first-rate, John admired Paul's knack for performing, his power to excite, to shade the music with his personality. It defined everything John was thinking about rock 'n roll. "From the beginning, Paul was a showman," said Pete Shotton. "He'd probably been a showman all his life."

· · · · ·

Paul owed much of this knack to his family's passion for music. His grandfather Joe, an Irish immigrant, loved opera and played the clunky double E-flat bass horn in a marching band that entertained regularly in a local park and at parades, and his father, Jim, a jovial man with a penchant for deadpan humor, pounded out popular songs on an old upright piano. On oppressively hot summer days that brought the city to an early boil, more than a dozen neighbors often congregated in the street below the McCartneys' parlor window and danced, to Jim's accompaniment, into the night.

Before he was twenty, Jim McCartney was already preoccupied with pop music. He would stumble home from work, stay just long enough for dinner, then hit the road, looking for a jam. During the early 1920s, he fronted his own band, the Masked Melody Makers, who wore mysterious black masks and played at small dance halls around Liverpool. Later, he led a smaller group called Jim Mac's Jazz Band. Nothing made him feel more carefree than music, and with his brother Jack, he stole off regularly to the neighborhood theaters to catch the latest music hall revues. "My father learned his music from listening to it every single night of the week, two shows every night," Paul recalled. It is easy to understand how this eventually influenced his son.

Even though Paul's mother, Mary, wasn't at all musical, she encouraged her family's passion. There was always music in the house, which delighted Mary, even when she craved precious sleep. Sleep was something she never got enough of, due to her demanding job as a midwife. Paul watched his mother depart at all hours of the day or night to assist in the home delivery of babies. When pressed into action, she'd throw her heavy nurse's bags over her bicycle, dump her purse into a wicker basket attached to the handlebars, and speed off into the dark like Batman, often not returning home in time for sleep.

Cycling around Liverpool was no waltz in the park. The hills surrounding the McCartneys' residence were steep. Incredibly, Mary never surrendered to them, despite the effects of a cigarette habit that left her gasping for breath. One road in particular, Fairway Street,

23

was the steepest in all of Liverpool, but Mary routinely scaled it, rain or shine. During the spring, Mary would be called out nearly every night, which was very stressful.

Sometime in 1946, when Paul was four, the family moved to Speke, a new, windswept suburb a few miles south of Liverpool, which seemed half a universe away. There was something delicious about leaving all that inner-city congestion behind. To an inquisitive child like Paul, Speke was a magical kingdom, with wide-open spaces and endless horizons. He enjoyed playing outside all day with his younger brother, Mike, who, according to a friend, "followed him like a puppy down every street." They were always off on a rousing bicycle adventure or hiking along a rise above the Mersey River, where they could see the entire northern coast and explore the old lighthouse that stood sentry for ships navigating around the channel. Other times, they climbed up Tabletop Bridge, where, lying in wait like superspies, they would pelt the onrushing trains with turnips scavenged in an adjacent field.

But their exuberance collapsed when it was discovered that Mary had cancer. By the time it was diagnosed, the disease was already in an advanced stage; cases like these, Mary knew, were almost always fatal. But instead of dwelling on it, she saved all her energy for her boys, who were a handful. She ran herself ragged trying to keep up with them.

Mary sensed she had little time left, and so she was determined to encourage the boys' schooling. She read poetry to her sons and insisted they cultivate an interest in books and ideas that would carry them far beyond the limitations of their parents' lives. Jim supported her every step of the way. An armchair philosopher, he

Young lads looking in the shop window at guitars for sale, Liverpool, 1964. © MIRRORPIX

The Everly Brothers. © Chuck Stewart/Redferns

Little Richard. © Michael Ochs Archives/Redferns

stressed the importance of principles, such as self-respect, perseverance, a relentless work ethic, and fairness. Most of all, he expected give-and-take. "He was a great conversationalist, very opinionated, an impassioned talker," said a nephew who recalled Jim's ritual of "matching wits" with Paul in an effort to provoke animated discussion.

Thanks to his parents' encouragement, Paul was admitted to the Liverpool Institute—known as "the Inny"—one of the city's elite schools, which sent as many students as possible to Oxford and Cambridge Universities. "The first year, I was pretty lost," Paul recalled. "But by the second year, I was learning Latin, Spanish, and German—at age twelve, which wasn't bad." Paul described his performance as "reasonably academic," but his grades fell consistently—and sharply—by the end of the third year.

By that point there were too many distractions, and for Paul, nothing in school could compete with a force like rock 'n roll.

Among Paul's mounting distractions was Radio Luxembourg's nighttime broadcast, which he listened to in bed via an extension-cord-and-headphone device that Jim had hooked up to the radio in the living room. Paul considered the broadcast "a revelation," and he began to mimic the voices that wailed across the airwaves. The raw, raunchy, and often ferocious intensity of Ray Charles, Ivory Joe Hunter, Hank Ballard, and Fats Domino riveted Paul, and Little Richard's extraordinary range would influence him throughout his career.

He desperately longed to sing like these recording artists. It was next to impossible, however, with a trumpet, which had been handed down to him by a cousin. He pleaded with his father to buy him a guitar, but Jim couldn't afford to spend three weeks' salary on such an extravagance, especially since Paul already had a perfectly good instrument. Finally, Paul asked permission to trade the trumpet for a guitar, and Jim gave in. Paul made a beeline for one of Liverpool's leading music stores, where he exchanged the trumpet for a crudely made Zenith guitar—a brown sunburst model with *f*-holes—that was propped against one of the shelves. The salesman must have struggled to conceal his delight at the deal; it wasn't every day he came by a trumpet worth five or six times the price of a guitar. All the same, he had no idea how pivotal that transaction would be.

A Sampling of a Beatles Early Rock 'n Roll Set

Kansas City (Wilbur Harrison)

Leave My Kitten Alone (Johnny Preston)

Heartbreak Hotel (Elvis Presley)

Cathy's Clown (The Everly Brothers)

Baby, It's You (The Shirelles)

Save the Last Dance for Me (The Drifters)

You've Really Got a Hold on Me
(Smokey Robinson & the Miracles)

To Know Him Is to Love Him (The Teddy Bears)

Soldier of Love (Arthur Alexander)

Roll Over Beethoven (Chuck Berry)

Honky Tonk Blues (Hank Williams)

Everybody's Trying to Be My Baby
(Carl Perkins)

Dizzy Miss Lizzy (Larry Williams)

Rip It Up (Little Richard)

"The minute he got the guitar, that was the end," Paul's brother, Mike, recalled. "He was lost. He didn't have time to eat or think about anything else."

Paul's lifelong romance with the guitar had begun, but from the outset he encountered

27

mechanical problems. Guitars were made for right-handed musicians, and Paul was left-handed. Most lefties learned how to play right-handed chord patterns or simply turned the guitar around so that the fingering was reversed. Neither method, however, worked for Paul. They intruded on his rhythm, leaving his arm sawing the air in stiff curves and tripping his timing like a broken switch. Yet Paul would not give up. It took him weeks to figure out how to lick the problem, but at last he discovered a solution: he restrung the guitar in reverse, so that the thinner, high-pitched strings were in the bass notes position, and vice versa. It was "all rather inexact," as Paul explained it later, but served to give him the control necessary to synchronize the rhythm with the mechanics.

· · · · ·

Paul wasn't alone in his struggle to master the instrument. Even before he got a guitar, John Lennon would pantomime playing one, striking poses in front of his bedroom mirror and stomping determinedly across

A teenage girl listens to a record played on an instore phonograph, London, 1956. © HULTON-DEUTSCH COLLECTION/CORBIS

the floor until his aunt Mimi ordered him to stop. He spent endless hours lip-synching to songs on the radio. From time to time, John took the bus into downtown Liverpool and stared longingly at the guitars in the window of Hessy's, a music store that carried the city's best selection of instruments. He begged Aunt Mimi for one, but she steadfastly refused, arguing that guitar playing "was of no worldly use" to him.

He turned to his mother, Julia, who was more disposed to the idea. During her daily visits to Mimi's house, John would bring up the subject, reminding her how much she herself enjoyed playing the banjo. But Mimi's objections posed a real dilemma. "Perhaps next year," Julia told her son, "when you are finished with school."

This was small comfort to John, who was determined to have his way, even if it meant playing the sisters against each other. He came across an advertisement in a magazine for an inexpensive guitar that was "guaranteed not to crack." All that separated him from owning it was £5, and after much pleading, Julia agreed to lend him the money on the condition that the instrument was delivered to her house instead of Mimi's. The steel-string guitar was called a Gallotone Champion, with a style that was part cowboy, part Spanish. "It was a bit crummy," John admitted later. But as guitars go, it was sturdy enough to hold a note, and he immediately began to wrestle with it to produce a consistent sound.

How Did the Beatles Find Fresh Material?

When the Beatles first began playing clubs in Liverpool, finding new, fresh material became John's most pressing goal and his greatest problem. Radio was the most accessible medium, but airplay at the time was still severely limited. The only radio station in the UK, the BBC, played little or no rock 'n roll. Sheet music was scarce, and the cost of records was prohibitive. The only other prospect was going to a record store, where it was possible to listen to one or two selections and try to write down the lyrics. So John and two friends would climb over the school wall at lunchtime and head to the North End Music Shop (or NEMS, as it was known). "You could listen to the odd record there in a booth," recalled a friend, "but then they threw us out when they realized we weren't buying anything."

John's friend Eric Griffiths also had a new guitar and convinced him to take a few lessons, but after two, John had had enough. There were too many rules, not enough payoffs. John wasn't interested in technique so long as he could strum a few chords and sing along. Instead, he convinced his mother to retune the guitar strings to the banjo and teach the boys banjo chords.

With that under their belts, John and Eric were soon working out their own informal arrangements. After school, they met at Mimi's and holed up in John's bedroom, where they tried learning, without much success, the rock 'n roll songs they heard on the radio. "We were [too] limited by the few chords [we knew]," Eric recalled. So they switched gears and tried something simpler. Playing skiffle, they tore through simple three-chord classics like "Rock Island Line," "Pick a Bale of Cotton," and "Cumberland Gap."

John threw himself into the practices. He was completely uninhibited about singing, belting out each number the way he imagined an entertainer would deliver it. "John was a born performer," Eric said. "You could sense that when he sang. It lifted him; he was energized by it."

Across the city, on the other side of Liverpool, Paul McCartney was caught up in the same kind of ritual. He was completely focused on the guitar, playing and singing to his heart's content. It was the only thing that mattered, "and so the academic things were forgotten," he remembered.

Mary tried to stay after him as best she could. Her goal was to groom Paul for university and afterward, she hoped, medical school. But her health was failing. The cancer was consuming her. Occasionally, she would yelp and double over, kneading her chest until the pain passed. But as the cancer spread, her stamina faded. Mary could barely get up the stairs to the bedroom without help. On October 30, 1956, she checked herself into the hospital. The next evening, Paul and Mike came to visit—for the last time, as it turned out. Mary suffered an embolism and died shortly after the boys left.

For weeks, Paul bumped around the house "like a lost soul." No one recalled ever seeing him sink so low. "I was determined not to let it affect me," he said. "I learned to put a shell around me at that age." To fill the gaps, Paul turned to music. He threw himself into playing the guitar, practicing chords and finger positions for hours on end, but not in any way that expressed a sense of pleasure. "It was the only way he could disengage himself from the tragedy," recalled his aunt.

Paul's grades, which had already been falling to a degree, slipped even further. He "skivved off" classes with alarming regularity and paid little attention to homework. In the midst of so much emotional turbulence, Paul reached out for a lifeline: rock 'n roll. Listening to it for long stretches, escaping into its defiant tone and lyrics, took him away from the painful memories.

Buddy Holly and the Crickets, Jerry Allison and Joe Maudlin, on the *Off the Record* television show, circa 1955. © Mirrorpix

Paul loved mimicking its nuances. Thanks to his ear for languages, it was easy for him to pick up the subtle inflections and shadings in the vocal performances. Buddy Holly, Elvis, Chuck Berry, Carl Perkins—they were all American rock 'n roll stars, and they had the magic, all right. He wanted to sound how they sounded, look how they looked, play how they played. Stretched across his bed, he would sink into a kind of dreamlike state, staring out the window, not looking at anything in particular, not even thinking, but lulled by the music's alchemy, hour after hour. At the center of his dreaming was the desire to do something more with music. What or with whom, he wasn't sure. But he sensed it was only a matter of time until it all came together and he put his own stamp on it.

Eight months later, he met John Lennon.

Chapter 3

Once Paul McCartney joined the Quarry Men, John's little engine of a band picked up steam. Still, Paul's debut appearance with them—on October 18, 1957—was a complete disaster. Determined to make an impression, Paul had been practicing relentlessly for the gig, but he was so nervous during a solo that he suffered an attack of butterfingers, missing key notes, and the whole arrangement caved in like a soufflé. John, who took great personal pride in the Quarry Men, was momentarily startled—and embarrassed. "I thought he was going to lay into [Paul] something fierce," recalled Colin Hanton, the group's drummer. But the pitiful sight of Paul looking so deflated cut right through any hard feelings. John laughed so hard he almost fell down.

The band was raw and amateurish, but that did nothing to brake the speed at which John and Paul's relationship was developing. The two boys spent part of every day together, talking about music. Often, after school or on a day off, John would invite Paul back to Mendips, where they would hole up in John's bedroom, playing records and running down bits of lyrics they'd memorized in an attempt to piece together entire songs. "We spent hours just listening to the stars we admired," John recalled. "When a record had ended, we'd try and reproduce the same sort of sound ourselves." Paul's pet expression for it—"just bashing around"—seems appropriate. They found ways to play songs using what little they knew about chord structure and technique.

Sometimes, when they sat in Paul's sun-filled living room, all their big dreams poured out: the kind of band they envisioned putting together, the musical possibilities that lay in

Young George Harrison playing the guitar, 1954.
© Michael Ochs Archives/CORBIS

store, the great possibilities if they worked hard. John talked, in fact, about playing serious gigs—even making records! Anyone eavesdropping might have written off these plans as teenage fantasies; still, other teenagers had managed to pull it off.

A rhythm developed between John and Paul that got stronger and tighter. They understood each other. "Once they got together, things became serious—and fast," recalled Eric Griffiths. "The band was supposed to be a laugh; now they devoted all their attention to it and in a more committed way than any of us really intended." In Colin Hanton's estimation, "The band quickly *became* John and Paul. Even when someone didn't turn up to rehearse, John and Paul would be at it, harmonizing or arranging material, practicing, either at Aunt Mimi's or at Paul's house."

No doubt about it, they were tuned to the same groove. Still, their personalities were different. Where John was impatient and careless, Paul was a perfectionist. Where John was moody and aloof, Paul was outgoing and irrepressibly cheerful. Where John was straightforward if brutally frank, Paul practiced diplomacy. Where John was struggling to become a musician, Paul seemed born to it. And John gave Paul someone to look up to. He had a style that awed people and set things in motion. "After a while, they'd finish each other's sentences," Eric Griffiths remembered. "That's when we knew how strong their friendship had become. They'd grown dependent on one another."

Thereafter, it was John and Paul who brought all the new material to the Quarry Men. They assigned each musician his part, they chose the songs—they literally dictated how rehearsals went down. "Say the wrong thing, contradict them, and you were frozen out," recalled Colin Hanton. "A look would pass between them, and afterwards it was as if you didn't exist."

Throughout the rest of the year, the two boys reinforced their collaboration. Paul especially began to distinguish himself on guitar. He had a real feel for the instrument, not just for strumming it but for subtle things like vamping on the strings with the heel of his hand and accenting chords with single bass notes. John's technique was more spontaneous, more relaxed. "He had a way of just banging out a few chords and making it sound cool," observed one of his friends. "Any song, no matter if he knew it or not—John would barrel right through it."

Sometime in late February, Paul began learning an instrumental called "Raunchy," playing the melody line over and over until it was nearly note-perfect. But there was more to it than simply learning the song. He had heard another boy play it, a fifteen-year-old schoolmate whom he had befriended two years earlier, and he wanted to master the song to maintain their friendly rivalry. He almost had it down, but it wasn't quite there yet. And not until it was dead-on would he play it for George Harrison.

• • • • •

Even before he met Paul McCartney, George Harrison had demonstrated that he was not to be outperformed when it came to the guitar.

One day when he was just thirteen years old, George and his best friend, Arthur Kelly, were practicing a version of a skiffle hit they'd learned from listening to a record. Because they'd only recently taken up the guitar, Arthur said, "We could barely switch chords, let alone do anything fancy." But when they got to the middle part, George lit into the difficult lead, galloping through the break, leaving Arthur dazzled. "We'd only heard the song two or three times, but George had somehow memorized it. He just inhaled those notes and played them back perfectly, at the same speed as on the record." As Arthur soon realized,

George was a natural when it came to the guitar.

As a teenager, the slight, spindly George Harrison was a detached, introspective boy with dark, expressive eyes, huge ears, and a mischievous smile that seized his whole face with a kind of wolfish delight. Although he was by no means a loner, he was outwardly shy, and it was the kind of shyness so inhibiting that it was often misinterpreted as arrogance. He tended to disappear within himself, to give away as little as possible. Friends from the neighborhood were less eloquent, remembering him as someone who "blended in with the scenery." George was "a quieter, more taciturn kind of guy" than other blokes, according to another acquaintance, "but he was pretty tough as well." There was nothing in his development that hinted at the witty, disarming Beatle whose spontaneous antics would transform press conferences into stand-up comedy.

Unlike Paul's family, the unworldly Harrisons offered George little in the way of academic enrichment, nothing that would jump-start a young man's imagination. Nor did they have the kind of high-toned pretensions that Mimi had for John. Like many of the hard-nosed port people who were resettled in the Liverpool suburbs in the 1930s, they were content just to enjoy their upgraded lifestyle—not to "rock the boat," in the wisdom of a Harrison family slogan—rather than to reach for the stars.

Like Freddie Lennon, George's father, Harry, had grown up around the Liverpool docks, enchanted by their gritty romance and faraway lure. By the age of seventeen, he was already trolling the seas for the fancy White Star Line, living between a series of exotic ports. He met George's mother, Louise, while on shore leave in Liverpool and married her the next year, struggling to stay afloat financially. The birth of two children—also named Harry and Louise—made things extremely difficult on twenty-five bob (shillings) a week, which was inadequate to support them.

It took almost two years of scraping by until Harry landed another job, working as a streetcar conductor and then driver on the Speke-Liverpool route. He loved bus driving from the first day he slipped behind the wheel, and in thirty-one years on the job, there was never a day in which he regarded it as anything but a sacred, businesslike obligation.

Within four years, the Harrisons had another boy, Peter, and then George was born, on February 25, 1943. He was an unnaturally beautiful child. Dark-haired and dark-eyed, with skin like polished bone and a lean-jawed face that favored his father's features, he quickly developed the kind of strong armor that protects the youngest sibling from getting constantly picked on.

The Harrisons were a boisterous crew—good-natured boisterous. "They'd yell at each other and swear around the [dinner] table," recalled Arthur Kelly. There was a good deal of taunting and ridiculing one another—none of which was expressed with any unpleasantness. In fact, Kelly said, he was envious of their noisy interaction, the earthy way they expressed their affections. "I enjoyed being there… because with all the uproar they were very much a family."

Liverpool ferries, 1954. © HULTON-DEUTSCH COLLECTION/CORBIS

Like Paul's family, the Harrisons moved from the city to Speke. Living in a suburb seemed fantastic to George because it meant space and a chance to develop his own identity. George couldn't have been happier. He went to nearby Dovedale Primary, which John Lennon had also attended, where he was a decent pupil with good manners, and he passed a scholarship exam with a good enough score to assure himself a coveted place in one of Liverpool's elite high schools. That alone was reason to celebrate in the Harrison family. George's father talked tirelessly about the importance of a good education and how hard work in school was the only way to escape a dreadful life of poverty and physical labor. None of George's siblings had their heart set on going to college, but George gave his father

a glimmer of hope that at least one of his children would go to college and make something of himself.

And while part of that dream would be fulfilled, it would be about as far from the halls of ivy as a boy could reasonably stray.

· · · · ·

Within weeks of entering the prestigious Liverpool Institute—the same school as Paul—George Harrison altered the course of his life in ways that no one could have predicted. He was marked for trouble from the start. Uncooperative, indifferent, and unmotivated in class, immature and stubborn to the point of rebelliousness, he was adrift in a school that stressed discipline and conformity. Already testing authority, George wore bold checkered shirts, pants that were so tight they were called "drainpipes," and blue suede shoes. His hair, which had grown extravagantly long—long enough for his father to label him "a refugee from a Tarzan movie"—was plastered back with palmfuls of gel to make it behave and topped with sugar water so that it would dry like Sheetrock. "Basically, George and I were a couple of outcasts," Arthur Kelly said. Sometimes George and Arthur simply "sagged off" school to smoke cigarettes and eat French fries in a nearby movie theater that played endless cartoons. "From about the age of thirteen," Kelly said, "all we were interested in was rock 'n roll."

George threw himself into music with the furious energy of someone trying to escape a terrible trap. According to Arthur Kelly, he took a few basic guitar lessons "from a bloke who lived around the corner," then formed a skiffle band, called the Rebels,

Arthur Kelly and George Harrison (age twelve), just days after George got his first guitar.
Courtesy of Arthur Kelly

with Kelly, mostly for laughs. It is no coincidence that his Radio Luxembourg favorites were the exact same songs that captivated John Lennon and Paul McCartney, with the exception that George was also drawn to guitarists whose twangy riffs were the bedrock of rock 'n roll tradition. He paid a lot of attention to the way these performers played, the phrasing and shading that made their songs so immediately recognizable.

Said Colin Manley, who with George was considered one of the best guitar players at the Liverpool Institute, "He knew how to color a riff, which none of us even considered trying to do before. It was so different, so inventive—and serious. It's difficult to understand how unusual that was at the time. Most of us wanted to just play that damn instrument, but George was out to conquer it." His success as a guitarist, Manley said, was due to hours of painstaking, monotonous practice bent over the frets. "He used to come over to my house, put a record on, and we'd play a passage over and over again until we'd mastered it. George studied guitar the way someone else would a scientific theory. And it challenged him in the same way."

A double-decker bus, 1956. © Hulton-Deutsch Collection/CORBIS

Unfortunately, George's grades plunged as he improved on guitar. He'd stopped studying altogether and concentrated solely on playing music. Only occasionally did he put in an appearance at school, and when he showed up at all, trouble followed. He had few friends there, but one he eventually made proved especially important.

As George recounted, "I'd met Paul on the bus, coming back from school," at the end of 1956. Paul shared George's interest in music, and the two spent afternoons practicing guitar. Most Liverpool Institute upperclassmen never mixed with the younger students, but for

George, with his interest in rock 'n roll and undeniable talent, Paul felt the affection of an older brother. He watched over George in school and dragged him along on a couple of social outings. But friends though they were, Paul kept his business with the Quarry Men quite separate. George heard only passing remarks about the band.

It wasn't until March 12, 1958, that George was invited to hear the Quarry Men at the opening of a skiffle club called the Morgue. George arrived carrying his beat-up guitar. Paul made introductions, and he could see from John's reaction that fifteen-year-old George was too young, "just a schoolkid." Paul was almost sixteen and John was seventeen, so the difference was huge as far as John was concerned. With little prompting, George pulled out his guitar and auditioned for the other boys. "The lads were very impressed," recalled Eric Griffiths. Colin Hanton said, "He played the guitar brilliantly—better than any of us handled an instrument—so I had no hang-up about inviting him to come around."

Maybe Hanton didn't, but John did. He wanted nothing to do with a mere schoolboy and told Paul so. "George was just too young," John recalled. "He looked even younger than Paul, and Paul looked about ten, with his baby face." Not to be denied, Paul, who thought George was loaded with talent, engineered another "chance" meeting between John and George in, of all places, the upper deck of a Liverpool bus. Once more, George had his guitar in tow, and this time he zipped through a rendition of another difficult song. There was no way for John to exclude him any longer: George Harrison was in the band.

Unfortunately, that spelled the end for Eric Griffiths and the other feeble guitar players who came around to play. There wasn't any room for them with a musician like George on board. As a result, the Quarry Men got very tight.

John, Paul, George—and Colin. They were almost there.

• • • • •

For almost a year after George joined the Quarry Men, living rooms and backyards were, in general, the only places in which the band played gigs. Though local dance halls and "jive" clubs actively booked acts to fill the demand for music, they showed little interest in hiring the boys.

Frustrated by the band's slow progress, John and Paul concentrated on practicing together every chance they got—and they hit upon a momentous discovery. Paul mentioned casually that he'd written several songs, and he played one for John, called "I Lost My Little Girl." John was, in one friend's estimation, "floored." Writing songs had never occurred to him.

Throughout the spring of 1958, John and Paul gave songwriting a try. Lo and behold, songs poured out of them at an extraordinary rate. They would begin by scrawling "A Lennon-McCartney Original" at the top of a blank sheet of paper, then jotted down anything they came up with: words, images, fragments of lyrics. Gradually, a verse would take shape, then another and another. "Lyrics didn't really count," John recalled, "as long as we had some vague theme: 'She loves you, he loves her, and they love each other.'"

By the end of the school year, a respectable number of original songs had been written down in a beat-up notebook. There were between fifteen and twenty in all, including "One After 909," "I Call Your Name," and "Love Me Do," all of which would eventually be recorded by the Beatles. John was attending the Liverpool College of Art, which was next door to the Liverpool Institute, so Paul and George spent lunch hours visiting him, playing in the college cafeteria. Usually, a small crowd would gather to listen. One of the students remembered being touched by the boys' developing talent. "They were wonderful," she said. "They harmonized just beautifully together. Everyone appreciated having them around."

One sweltering-hot night in June, they played at a dinner dance, and John's mother turned up. John had been badgering her to hear the band for some time. Julia was "absolutely overwhelmed" at the sight of John cutting loose on the stage, a guest remembered. "She couldn't stop moving" to the music, and between the numbers she was "the only person," said Colin Hanton, "who clapped every time—and *loud*. If that didn't get things going, she put her fingers in her teeth and whistled." She seemed genuinely proud of John and thrilled by his band.

Even though John lived at Aunt Mimi's, he continued to see his mother on a regular basis. The two spent long hours together, discussing everything from school to music. For all her inadequacies as a mother, Julia had a wonderful sense of dealing with a teenager. Things were also getting better between Julia and Mimi. The sisters were unfailingly loyal to each other, and Julia visited Mimi each day. They would usually have a cup of tea in Mimi's morning room, adjacent to the kitchen, but in warmer weather they often stood in the garden and talked, sometimes lingering into the early evening.

It was there that Nigel Walley, John's friend and manager, found them on July 15, 1958, chatting across the garden gate. "I'd gone around to call for [John]," Nigel remembered. "It was a beautiful summer night, just getting dark. But, as it turned out, he wasn't home." Julia was about to leave, and Nigel offered to walk her as far as the bus stop. Sauntering down the sidewalk, Julia cracked joke after joke. When they got to the intersection, Nigel waved good-night and turned toward home. Julia crossed the avenue in the middle of the block. Seconds later, Nigel heard a screech of tires, followed by a hideous thud, and saw Julia flying through the air. For a split second, the whole world froze. Nigel tried to scream but "couldn't get a sound out." He ran toward where Julia had fallen, but he could see "she wasn't moving."

It was just after eleven o'clock when a patrol car pulled up in front of Julia's house, where John was. A policeman stood stiffly on the front step, his face frozen in sorrow as he told John that his mother was dead. John was consumed with grief. Thoughts of his past, of his absent father, mingled with thoughts of the present. "That's really [ruined] everything," he thought. "I've got no responsibility to anyone now." The way John saw it, "I lost my mother twice—once as a five-year-old…and again when she actually, physically died."

It was logical that John would bury his sorrow in the band. "Now we were both in this, both losing our mothers," Paul later said. "This was a bond for us, something of ours, a special thing." In a way, Paul was right. From that day onward, he and John formed a mutual, unspoken understanding, bound by their respective sadness.

43

One of the band's few joys the next year was playing at the art college dances, which were held on Friday nights in the basement canteen. Students who recall those evenings still talk about the thrill of hearing rock 'n roll ringing off the canteen's bare concrete walls. Said one observer: "It was as new and disturbing as anything we'd heard at school. [The Quarry Men] had a sound that just connected with us, and when that band played, the place went wild."

But Paul wasn't satisfied, and neither was John. They were getting better by playing with George, but Colin wasn't. And he didn't fit in with their developing friendship. Paul, the perfectionist, blamed Colin for dragging the band down. After one gig, playing at a social club, there was an argument between the boys that ended badly. Colin took his drums home, saying he'd see them at the next gig. But there was no next gig, and no phone call from any of the Quarry Men. "In fact, I never saw them again," Colin said, "until three years later, when I turned on the television and some guy was going on about a band called the Beatles."

· · · · ·

Adrift without a drummer, George, Paul, and John spent many nights listening to and studying the young bands in Liverpool that were getting all the work. Helplessly, they sat idle while the local music scene grew up and around them. Everywhere they turned, the rock 'n roll bandwagon was rumbling ahead. Teen clubs opened as fast as promoters could find vacant buildings to rent. Other bands worked four or five nights a week, but without a drummer, the Quarry Men couldn't play gigs. For all intents and purposes, they were finished.

For John, who had loved the band most, it was another emotional setback. His mother was dead; his best friend, Pete Shotton, had become preoccupied with police cadet training. And a neighborhood girlfriend had thrown in the towel and taken up with another young man. All of this brought John's feeling of alienation into sharper focus. His friendships with two college classmates, Bill Harry and Stuart Sutcliffe, helped, although both students, unlike John, were committed to their art. Aside from Paul and George, there seemed to be no one to fill the void. His entire support system was falling apart.

Then, a few days before the end of the school term, Cynthia Powell walked into his life.

· · · · ·

It had never occurred to Cynthia that the "scruffy, dangerous-looking, and totally disruptive" boy who "frightened the life out" of her at art college would end up her soul mate. John Lennon was a character out of her worst nightmares, "outrageous...a rough sort" who flew so far below her social radar that his existence barely registered.

They had been in class together for most of the year, but as the girl from the studious side of the aisle, Cynthia Powell had escaped special notice. Painfully timid, she melted into crowds like the scenery in an unfocused photograph. She was slim and delicately shaped, with good legs and a smile that puckered slightly, but her beauty was a gift she ignored.

It was almost by accident that Cynthia came to John's attention. They were in a lettering class together, but, as Cynthia recalled, "For John...[lettering] was impossible." In order to distract from his inability, he became the class cutup, the clown. Still, this bad boy who disrupted everything he came into contact with lit a fire in her, and

Cynthia and John, 1964. © MIRRORPIX

45

they struck up a "vague friendship."

Later that December, a few days before the end of term, Cynthia and a group of friends decided to celebrate the upcoming holiday by going to a hangout between classes. After lunch, everyone drifted back to school, where an impromptu party was already in progress. A record player had been set up in one of the rooms. When John pushed his way through a tangle of couples and asked her to dance, she fell rapturously into his arms.

She came away from that room, Cynthia said, "madly in love." For the next few weeks, John and Cynthia were just about inseparable. Their attraction may have shocked their fellow students, who considered the two of them "like chalk and cheese," but it was mostly regarded with enthusiasm and relief. John became less of a cutup and easier to be around. "It calmed him down," recalled a friend, "letting us live and learn in peace."

But there was still music and the band that needed resolving, and until that score was settled, there would be no peace in John Lennon's young life.

• • • • •

By the end of 1958, without much happening with John and Paul, George's desire to play was so strong that he took up with three other friends who had a rock 'n roll band. They had arranged to play at the opening of a new club called the Casbah, which was in the basement of a large, handsome house owned by a family named Best. One of George's bandmates knew Pete Best from school. It had been Pete who convinced his mother, Mona, to invite kids to dance in their basement and to put in special lights and a sound system. More than three hundred teenagers had already purchased club membership cards, so the opening promised to be a very special event.

A week before the Casbah opened, however, the band fell apart. George was on his way to the Bests' house to give them the bad news when a friend asked him if there was any way to salvage the job. He said he had two friends—John and Paul—and went off on a bus to fetch them.

46

For the moment, the Quarry Men were back in business. The Casbah was a runaway success. The new club was dazzling, hot, loud, young, private, and rocking—pulsing with just the right atmosphere. And the Quarry Men brought the house down. Even without a drummer, the kids loved them. Mona Best was so delighted that she guaranteed the band the princely sum of £3 a night to play there every Saturday. The Quarry Men were the featured attraction, and because of them the Casbah membership spiraled into the thousands. The club became so popular and crowded that after a while, you could barely hear the band. Eventually, however, an argument over money cost the Quarry Men their job, and a new band took over, featuring Pete Best, who had recently taken up the drums.

· · · · ·

Throughout the next school year, in 1959–60, things became very hectic for John, Paul, and George. John grew bored with his college studies; impatient as ever, he hated *learning* about art as opposed to actually painting and drawing. Besides, he was pre-

Pete Best on drums, 1962. © K&K STUDIOS/REDFERNS

47

Stuart Sutcliffe and George, who became good friends, sharing a quiet and thoughtful musical interlude, 1960. © PETER BRUCHMANN/REDFERNS

occupied with rock 'n roll, so there was little to hold his attention in the classroom. George was also having trouble concentrating and eventually quit school. "At that stage, he didn't have any idea what he wanted to do with his life," recalled his friend Arthur Kelly. Everyone seemed to have a suggestion, but George was content to take a job at one of Liverpool's department stores until something better came along. Only Paul stuck it out in school, but even he was growing restless, and it showed in his dwindling grades.

Only rarely were the boys able to play somewhere meaningful as a band. There were very few gigs for a group without a drummer. Instead they entered several competitions, where they performed in a lineup with eight or ten other acts all hoping to be noticed by local promoters. Determined to break cleanly with the past, the Quarry Men changed their name to, of all things, Johnny and the Moondogs, which had the right touch of playful humor.

In the meantime, they continued to practice and play together, rehearsing at the flat of John's friend Stuart Sutcliffe. Stuart, a slight, gentle young man, was one of the most respected painters at the art college, brimming with talent and a promising future. In fact, he had just won first prize in a prestigious competition sponsored by the local art museum and had been awarded a considerable sum for the honor. John, who was always thinking of his band, knew exactly how his friend should spend it. "Now that you've got all this money, Stu," he said, "you can buy a bass and join our group."

It took only a long moment for Stuart to mull over the offer before responding to John. He thought it was a wonderful idea, even though he didn't know how to play a bass guitar or if he could carry a tune. It didn't matter. To Stuart, playing the bass was simply another form of art. "And anyway," he explained to a friend, "the band is going to be the greatest. I want to be part of it."

After Stuart joined the band, a more proper name seemed in order. One night in February 1960, while sitting around the flat, John and Stuart brainstormed to come up with something better than Johnny and the Moondogs. Both boys loved Buddy Holly and the Crickets, whose songs were an inspiration. John remembered "just thinking about what a good name the Crickets would be for an English group, when the idea of beetles came into my head." It was John's idea to change the spelling "to make it look like beat music, just as a joke," although when they printed it on a card to show the other boys, it became Beatals.

Paul and George heard about the new name the next day, and they immediately liked it. *The Beatals.* It had the right sound to it, they thought, amusing and cheeky. Yes, the Beatals—it would do nicely, everyone agreed.

But even with a name like the Beatals, the band was not able to attract any work. There was still the problem of the drums. And while Stuart looked swell with an electric bass slung across his body, there was the matter of actually *playing* it that needed to be worked out. Stuart's thumb plucked at the chunky strings, but he was able to produce little more than a steady heartbeat, a monotonous *thunk-thunk-thunk*. And it left his hands—those delicate instruments that produced such gorgeous paintings—in terrible shape.

The four boys, the Beatals, would rehearse for hours in the basement of a tiny Liverpool coffeehouse, the Jacaranda, where other art students were inclined to drop in and listen to them play. The coffeehouse's owner, Allan Williams, took an immediate interest in the band. He even encouraged the more professional local bands to include the Beatals in their get-togethers. One popular singer, Brian Casser—whom everyone called Cass—convinced them to change their name to the Silver Beetles. And a few days later he found them a drummer named Tommy Moore. Tommy was twice their age and had a day job operating a forklift, but he played in dance bands and could put the beat in the right place.

Now that they had a drummer, Stuart stayed after Allan Williams about giving the Silver Beetles a break. They were desperate to get going, to play in front of an audience. It didn't take long for Williams to get the band some action. A British rock star named Billy Fury was preparing a tour, and he agreed to take a Liverpool group as his backup band. Four of the city's best groups were invited to audition—as well as the Silver Beetles. The boys were beside themselves with joy, but it was clear to most people that they didn't stand a chance against the other, more professional bands. "We didn't even know them," said a musician who played with the flashy Seniors, "and I don't think anybody else knew them either."

The day of the audition—May 10, 1960—everyone crowded into a tiny club where Billy Fury sat stone-faced, listening to the competition. Cass's band, the Cassanovas, played first and did horribly. The Seniors, who followed them, sounded shrieky and shrill. Gerry and the Pacemakers sounded great, but they lacked a certain spark. And Cliff Roberts and the Rockers couldn't compete in any category. The Silver Beetles, who played last, had nothing to lose. The boys launched into a brilliant set that left the others in the dust. "They blew everyone away," recalled a musician who was there.

Billy Fury immediately cued his manager that the Silver Beetles were a natural fit. The manager wasn't so sure, but he agreed to take the boys as Fury's backing group—only *without* the bass player, Stuart. John stepped forward and turned him down cold. As far as the Silver Beetles were concerned, he explained, it was an all-or-nothing proposition. Either all of them went on tour or he could choose another band. In the end, it was decided that no Liverpool band would back Billy Fury. But another pop star, Johnny Gentle, who was about to begin a tour of Scotland, needed a backup band, and that job was offered instead to the boys.

The Silver Beetles were ecstatic. Johnny Gentle was an up-and-coming recording star, and this was a legitimate tour. They would finally have work as a real band.

Hastily, arrangements were made. Tommy Moore and George took time off from their jobs, Paul sweet-talked his father into a vacation before his upcoming exams, and Stuart and John simply cut classes. All the pieces fell neatly into place. Suddenly, everything seemed possible. They were actually going on the road—a road from which they would never look back.

Chapter 4

If the Silver Beetles had any illusions that life on the road was a glamorous one, they ended with the tour of Scotland.

For two weeks that summer in 1960, the boys crisscrossed hundreds of lonely miles through some of the most rugged, grim, and barren countryside on the northeast coast. There were none of the modern conveniences that cushioned travel between cities like Liverpool and London. The rickety train, lurching on the tracks, was insufferably hot and depressing, the stale air bone-dry and hard to breathe. It seemed to take forever to get to Scotland, as they snaked past the stagnant little provincial towns that dotted the river banks.

Johnny Gentle was waiting for them when they arrived. Though not yet quite a star, he had a decent following of fans who knew his two hit records and were waiting to see him perform. The Silver Beetles had only a half hour to rehearse with him and hammer out an agreeable set of songs before they were due to go on stage. They needed enough material for two one-hour shows, which meant they would have to work out most of it on the spot, in front of an audience.

They went right to work, playing at "border dances," which were social gatherings in little halls that held up to three hundred teenagers who could shuttle between upstairs rooms featuring rock 'n roll shows and downstairs auditoriums where traditional bands played the Scottish reel. Inside those dinky, dilapidated halls, the Silver Beetles pulled out all the stops. They pummeled those Scottish kids with forty minutes of the most exciting music that never let up for a beat. One after another, the songs built to a furious, undisciplined pitch, rumbling and wailing like a train through a tunnel. The kids at each show were undone by the music, practically throwing themselves around the floor.

"I used to watch [the Beatles] work the crowd as though they'd been doing it all their lives," Johnny Gentle remembered, "and without any effort other than their amazing talent. I'd never seen anything like it. [John and Paul] were so tapped into what each other was doing and could sense their partner's next move. They just read each other like a book." Johnny Gentle put on a good performance, and the fans loved him, but the Silver Beetles rose mightily to steal the whole show.

George Harrison, Stuart Sutcliffe, and John Lennon, photographed by Astrid Kirchherr, 1960. © K&K Ulf Kruger OHG/Redferns

The boys were naturals. Still, it was difficult work. They played until very late each night in front of notoriously rough crowds that often started fights during the shows. It was impossible to get to sleep before dawn. And there was very little money to be made. Three days into the tour, in a town called Fraserburgh, the last scrap of land on the gusty northeast coast of Scotland, the Silver Beetles' pockets were empty. They had to borrow money from Johnny Gentle so they could eat.

When they got back to Liverpool, the boys were tired and broke. But word had filtered back that they'd been brilliant on stage, so Allan Williams was able to book them for a string of dances that ran through the summer. The gigs helped to establish them locally, and they were paid an awesome £10 a night, more than they'd ever made before. The bad news was that the dances were in the worst holes this side of the equator—very rough ballrooms where punch-ups interrupted each song, with flying crates and beer bottles and glasses. The Silver Beetles learned how to play in any situation.

When it seemed they were about to hit the big time, Tommy Moore quit the band. The boys were devastated, though they tried to keep up appearances. Unable to play the rest of the summer dances without a drummer, they bumped around the city, singing in dingy pubs. But they were miserable, embarrassed, and depressed—an indication of how badly their dreams had stalled.

Just when everything seemed hopeless, just when it seemed they would have to disband and take up ordinary part-time jobs, Allan Williams threw them another life preserver. Williams had booked Derry and the Seniors, a popular Liverpool band, into a club in Hamburg, Germany, where British and American servicemen were stationed and where the demand for live music far exceeded the supply. The Seniors proved such a success that the promoter begged Williams to send him another Liverpool band to play in a second club he owned. Allan offered the gig to Rory Storm and the Hurricanes, whose drummer was a bearded character named Ringo Starr, but they were determined to finish an engagement in Wales. Instead, he flirted with the idea of sending the Silver Beetles. Reluctantly. "They were really in no condition to perform," recalled their friend Bill Harry, "but they courted Allan, and Stuart came on strong."

Once again, fate intervened. With nowhere to play, John, Paul, Stuart, and George just hung out in local coffee shops and dance clubs, scouting out the competition. One of their stops was at the Casbah, where, at the time, the Blackjacks were playing. Sitting behind the drums was Pete Best. As far as the Silver Beetles could tell, he was pretty good—"a real pounding rock 'n roll drummer," according to a fellow musician—and gave off "a powerful effect." He owned an impressive new drum kit, and it also didn't hurt that he looked good. Pete was a pale, stiff boy with a dusty mop of hair, eyelids all but shuttered, and an affecting

The Fifth Beatle

Throughout the Beatles' existence, several people claimed that they were "the Fifth Beatle." Murray the K, the New York disc jockey who greeted the boys when they first arrived in America and coined the phrase, was the first to stake his claim. But before Murray, there were other, more worthy candidates:

Stuart Sutcliffe: The Beatles' first bass player helped name the band and was the first to comb his bangs over his forehead.

Pete Best: The Beatles' original drummer gave them their powerful "atomic" sound and carried the beat throughout their apprenticeship in Hamburg.

Neil Aspinall: Their trusty roadie was with them from the beginning and remained with the band until they broke up in 1970. Today, he continues to serve as the president of Apple Music.

George Martin: Their distinguished producer mentored the Beatles through the recording process and deserves credit for allowing them to experiment with sound and establish their identity.

Brian Epstein: Their manager believed in them when others only laughed at the prospect of the Beatles' becoming "bigger than Elvis."

languid smile, and girls were drawn to him in a visceral way. The Silver Beetles were keenly interested. With a drummer like Pete, they'd surely convince Allan Williams to give them the Hamburg gig.

The only thing left to do was to poach Pete from the Blackjacks, which turned out to be child's play. Paul called him later that night, dangling a job opportunity that would pay him a whopping £15 a week. Pete didn't hesitate to accept. "I'd always liked them very much," he allowed of the Beatles. Besides, he dreaded going to a teachers college in the fall. "I decided [instead] to persevere with the music."

In the meantime, the other boys set about untangling personal commitments. John learned that he would not be welcomed back at the art college, where he was failing most of his courses. If Aunt Mimi found out, he'd never hear the end of it. Anyway, there was nothing she could do to keep John from going to Germany. He was nineteen, of legal age, and well outside his aunt's grasp. Paul had another term left at the Liverpool Institute and a father for whom education was the one sure route to social betterment. "I didn't want to go back

One of the Beatles' awkward Hamburg stage arrangements, with Paul stationed at the piano while Stuart anchored the bass. © K&K Studios/Redferns

to school, or college," Paul later explained. Yet he knew that Jim would not tolerate idleness. So Paul invited Allan Williams to the house to help plead his case. Allan laid it on thick, assuring Jim that there would be no problems, that he would look after the boys. And Paul probably implied that after Hamburg, he would continue his studies. Before the evening was over, Jim had given his consent.

Allan also spoke to Stuart Sutcliffe's parents. George had already dropped out of school and was free to do as he pleased. So the deal was sealed. Very quickly thereafter, the gears began to crank. Birth certificates were produced, along with passports and visas. Bags and equipment were packed and labeled for transit. It all came together with remarkable speed. On August 16, 1960, the Beatles (they finally changed the spelling of the name)—John, Paul, George, Stuart, and Pete—left for Hamburg.

George at the Star-Club, 1962. © K&K Studios/Redferns

· · · · ·

The Beatles had been out of England before—to Scotland, which they considered a pleasant enough place. But Germany was a different world altogether. Maybe even a different planet.

Hamburg itself was as familiar as their own backyard. A port with a thriving shipping trade conducted under a blanket of perpetual fog, it not only looked, felt, and smelled like Liverpool, the cafés even served a typical sailors' stew that was cooked back home. But the St. Pauli district, where they would play, resembled a carnival midway, only gaudier and more vulgar. The action was shoulder-to-shoulder, back-to-back: bars, nightclubs, cafés, luncheonettes, clip joints, arcades, dance halls, saloons. And lights—miles of lights—blazed with dizzying intensity. Floodlights lit up the sky; arc lamps washed the street in a strange glow. Here it was bright around the clock.

"It was an 'anything goes' kind of place," recalled a fellow musician who also played in Hamburg, "kind of a Dodge

City of the open seas." Hamburg looked just right to the Beatles, who could hardly believe their eyes. But the club, called the Indra, depressed them. It was a lounge—a girlie lounge— where bleary-eyed tourists sat glumly sipping beer. "We were crestfallen when we saw it," recalled Pete Best. Still, there was hope. All the place needed was a hot British band to generate some buzz, and the owner had been assured the Beatles were up to the job.

The Beatles knew what to play. John, Paul, and George were a walking encyclopedia of rock 'n roll songs. They could put together an hour's worth of material without repeating a song. But somehow their performances didn't click with the crowd. As far as creating excitement went, the Beatles weren't cutting it. They were as stiff as the customers who trickled into the club. They had no act to speak of, knew nothing of stagecraft, and as performers they weren't terribly engaging. What's more, the Beatles were required to play a staggering four and a half hours each night, six hours on weekends. That meant coming up with new material, not to mention the stamina.

"C'mon boys," Allan Williams exhorted them after the club owner issued a complaint, "make a show!"

Make a show! It was like something a teacher might say before the start of school speech day or a class play. *Make a show:* it sounded completely inappropriate for rock 'n roll. John couldn't stop snickering. He lurched around the stage in mock theatrics, diving toward the mike and duckwalking or dropping into a split. Allan, who didn't realize that John was goofing on him, cheered on the antics. "That's it! Make a show! Make a show!"

The German club owner also took up the chant, barking at the band in his comic accent, *"Mach Schau! Mach Schau!"*

The Beatles thought it was a scream. *"Mach Schau!"* The entire band got into the act, imitating John's happy horseplay. Paul raised his guitar, fencing with John. George chimed in, stamping and scrabbling his feet like a crazed Cossack. Stuart contorted his body as though dodging bullets. A cyclone of rhythmic unrest swept across the Indra, synced to Pete's ferocious beat.

It was the breakthrough the band needed. They were in perpetual motion, and in no time they transformed their sorry act into something exciting. Word spread quickly around St. Pauli that the Beatles were all the rage, and crowds thronged to the Indra to check out the newest British sensation. According to a Hamburg teenager who spent his weekends in St. Pauli, "There was no place else in the district that offered such an exciting selection of live music."

Even though there were breaks planted at forty-five-minute intervals, there was really never any letdown until well after two in the morning. And the breaks were

merely breathers. From their opening chords, the Beatles let it rip. All-out rockers soon filled every minute of the set. Paul and John combined to sing a steady string of songs that set a blazing pace. They really turned it on—and up—squeezing all they could out of their two tiny amps. It wasn't unusual for Pete Best to crawl into place behind his drum set only to have John or Paul whisper, "Crank it up, Pete, we're really going for it tonight." After a long night's work jackknifing across the stage to wild applause, the boys were so pumped up it usually took several hours before they were calm enough to

go to bed. Often they didn't get to sleep until four or five in the morning.

The Beatles worked like mad. They were so good, the club owner moved them across the street to his showplace, the Kaiserkeller, where they shared the stage with Rory Storm and the Hurricanes. From the opening night, October 4, 1960, the two bands commandeered the stage with a red-hot, rough-and-tumble force. For more than seven uninterrupted hours the bands churned out a string of high-octane rockers that left the capacity crowds in a sweaty, beer-soaked frenzy. "Every night was another amazing jam fest," recalled Johnny "Guitar" Byrne, who played lead for the Hurricanes. "The music got everyone so cranked up, and the whole place just shook, like Jell-O."

Every night it got louder and longer—seven o'clock in the evening until five in the morning. "Marathon sessions," as the two bands mutually termed them, with a very friendly rivalry serving to fatten the stakes.

The audiences were rough, much rougher than back home, but the Beatles still made friends, particularly three young German art students who cast a striking presence in the crowd. Stuart was immediately drawn to them. He admitted that it was "extremely difficult to take my eyes off them," especially the woman, whose name was Astrid Kirchherr, a strong and willowy blond beauty with a full tank of attitude. "I had never met anyone like them," Stuart recalled.

The attraction was mutual. "We were totally fans, totally in awe," recalled Jürgen Vollmer, one of Astrid's male companions. "[The Beatles] looked absolutely astonishing. My whole life changed in a couple minutes."

They watched the Beatles play almost every night of the week, sitting where they knew the band would see them. Astrid, who was a capable photographer, offered to take pictures of the group. The Beatles eagerly accepted. After the first photo session, she took them back to her home, where her mother made the boys dinner. Almost from the start, Stuart was infatuated with her. He began spending all available time with Astrid—and less time with the band. This sowed resentment with the others. John, Paul, and George were devoted to their music and practiced every spare moment they had. Even Pete Best contributed to their developing sound with his pounding drums. Stuart, on the other hand, had no innate feel for music. When it came to playing the bass, he was basically inept, eternally an amateur. Paul, who was a perfectionist, called Stuart the "weak link." It troubled John as well, but he was unwilling to say or do anything that might hurt his friendship with Stuart. At first. But as time wore on, even John grew disenchanted with Stu's playing.

Just when it seemed as if they had to do something about the situation, destiny intervened. A new bigger, better, and brassier club called the Top Ten opened around the corner from where they were playing. The Beatles began hanging out—and eventually playing in raucous jam sessions—there. This infuriated the owner of the Kaiserkeller. He wanted them for himself, felt they owed him loyalty. After the Top Ten offered the Beatles a job, the Kaiserkeller's owner fired them on the spot. George Harrison, who was still seventeen and underage, was deported by the police. "So I had to leave [Germany]," he said. "I had to go home on my own."

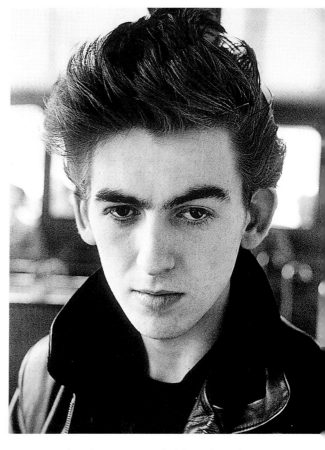

George Harrison in a young, and ultimately underage, portrait during the Beatles' first residency in Hamburg, 1960. © Jürgen Vollmer/Redferns

Before he left for Liverpool, George worked frantically to teach John the lead guitar parts to their songs so the Beatles could continue to function as a band. But it did them absolutely no good. When the remaining Beatles moved to the Top Ten, the owner of the Kaiserkeller took his revenge, accusing them of trying to burn down one of his buildings. It was a ridiculous charge, but the police were not amused. They arrested Paul and Pete and deported them as well.

John and Stuart remained in Hamburg, but without work permits it was impossible for them to earn a living. Besides, there was no one left to play with. John stayed only long enough to bum money for a train ticket home; Stuart borrowed airfare from Astrid and drifted home several weeks later.

The Beatles arrived back in Liverpool exhausted, broke, and greatly disillusioned. The incredible adventure was over. Meanwhile, each of the boys had to do some fancy explaining to his parents, to whom he'd boasted about fame and riches before setting off for Hamburg. John was completely depressed about their situation. George, too, said he "felt ashamed." He looked for work, as did Paul, who took a menial job at his father's insistence. For several weeks afterward, none of the boys touched base with one another. It seemed pointless. They weren't saying as much, but each of the Beatles was convinced that the band was finished.

• • • • •

A week before Christmas 1960, Pete phoned George and suggested they comb Liverpool for potential gigs. A few days later, they were joined by John, who was also eager to jump-start the Beatles' stalled career.

Through Allan Williams, the boys met a disc jockey named Bob Wooler, who emceed at all the local rock 'n roll halls and helped young bands get work. Bob was drawn to the Beatles. He sensed their awesome complexity and ambition and thought they emanated heat, signaling some kind of raw, restless talent. Purely on instinct, he decided to book them onto a few important shows during the holiday season, where they were seen by large groups of kids. The Beatles took everyone by surprise. They had changed drastically from when they had last played in Liverpool. Everything about them was different—their look, their sound, their poise. According to one observer, their performance was "a revelation to behold." No one had ever heard a local band play that hard before. Or look that rugged, in the black leather suits they'd bought in Hamburg. "To act that way on stage and

64

make that kind of sound," recalled Billy J. Kramer, who would one day record some of John and Paul's songs, "—I was absolutely staggered."

Word spread swiftly through Liverpool that the Beatles were the "must-see" band. Even without Stuart, who had stayed behind in Germany with Astrid, the band worked steadily, even furiously, at the plentiful number of dates available each week. They played somewhere almost every night, occasionally doubling up gigs and commuting between them at a dizzying, exhilarating pace. "For the first time people were following us around," George noticed, "coming to see us personally, not just coming to dance."

Then, in early 1961, their most important job came through. The Cavern, a Liverpool jazz showcase, was a filthy, sweltering, fetid, claustrophobic little firetrap of a club. It was located three stories below ground, in the cellar of an old warehouse that smelled foul and musty from its lack of ventilation. It was insufferably hot; the walls and ceiling sweated absolute humidity. And with eight hundred to a thousand teenagers sardined into a space fit for six hundred, it was an accident waiting to happen. But, oh, what a place to hang out, hear music, and dance! The cellar was in three sections separated by stone archways. The acoustics were great, and the crowd could see the stage from practically anywhere in the club.

The Cavern had always been a jazz only place, but by the end of 1960 its bookers could no longer ignore the

The classic Cavern stage shot, under the club's distinct brick archway.
© Michael Ward/Rex Features

65

YEAH! **YEAH! YEAH!**

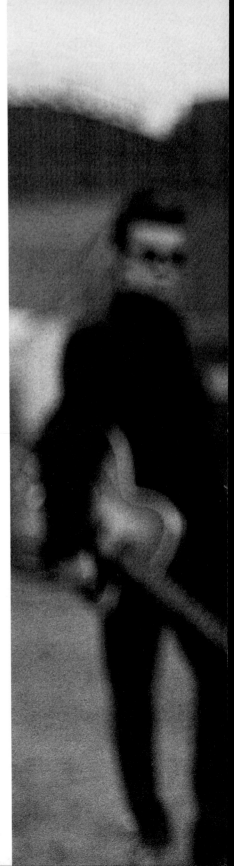

popularity of rock 'n roll, which created opportunities for local beat groups. The Beatles had been dying to play there. Its fussy owner, however, had other ideas and refused their advances. After Bob Wooler became the Cavern's resident deejay, he convinced the owner to give the Beatles a shot at one of the lunchtime sessions.

The Beatles debuted at the Cavern on February 21, 1961, playing to a solidly packed house. Their performance, loud and rocking, made an incredible impact on the club's regulars and sent the band's stock soaring. The audience loved what the Beatles had: stage presence and personality in addition to a great sound. The girls locked into it right away, and the boys soon followed suit. Even the club owner caught the vibe, sending word through Bob Wooler that the band was welcome back at the first opportunity.

Suddenly the Beatles were in great demand; work was everywhere. Each fabulous performance led to further offers. Paul and George were earning more money than their fathers, and while Aunt Mimi continued to badger John about certain failure (anything other than school meant failure to Aunt Mimi), she couldn't have been too disapproving of his £25-per-week income. Everything was going their way. Becoming rock 'n roll stars and making records were still the ultimate goals, but for the time being there was plenty of action to groove on.

• • • • •

Even with their careers on the upswing, the Beatles longed to return to Hamburg. They had loved playing there; the scene was so crazy and fabulous. At first, it seemed as though there were too

Paul photographed by Astrid Kirchherr, with the ghostly image of Stuart in the background, Hamburg, 1960. © ASTRID KIRCHHERR/REDFERNS

The Top Ten Club in Hamburg. © Helmut Uckermann/Redferns

many obstacles in their path for another visit, but one by one they began to disappear. Stuart got back to Hamburg first and announced his intention to marry Astrid Kirchherr. A few weeks later, the other Beatles followed with a promise of work at the Top Ten—seven hours a night, seven nights a week.

The Top Ten was a definite step up from the Kaiserkeller, with a great sound system and jam-packed crowds. Pretty soon the Beatles were the talk of the town. People stood in long lines outside the club, waiting to hear them play. The sound they put out was "amazing," recalled a regular, "unlike anything Hamburg ever heard before—or since."

This new popularity gave the Beatles confidence and allowed them to experiment with new roles and identities. Of all the Beatles, Stuart was most open to new experiences. He was the first to put on flamboyant clothes. And when he showed up at the Top Ten one night sporting a flashy new haircut, it set off a bomb in the Hamburg music world that resonated for years to come. The style was a takeoff on the "French cut," combed long across the forehead in soft, sculpted bangs. Astrid had styled it for Stuart. Out of ignorance—or envy—the other Beatles responded to his new haircut with childish insults. But two days later, a hesitant George followed suit, brushing his hair into an informal shaggy mop, and like that, the mold for the Beatle haircut was born.

Stuart helped set the trends, but all was not well between him and the other Beatles. "Paul hated Stu," recalled Dot Rhone, who went out with Paul. In fact, everything Stuart did now seemed to enrage him. There were many reasons for it. For one thing, Stuart had little musical talent and was slowing the band's progress. Then there were the hair and the clothes. Paul couldn't stand the way Stuart's fashion style hogged the spotlight. But most of all he was jealous of Stuart, especially his friendship with John. Finally, unable to take it anymore, Paul had it out with Stuart, not in private but on stage, in the middle of a set, in full view of an astonished German crowd. The fight, which had been brewing for months, was wild and fierce. The two boys rolled around on the floor, punching and stomping each other, while the other Beatles played on until the song ended, at which point John, George, and Pete pried them apart.

The Fashion of the Beatles

By 1965, the whole of London was moving to the beat of the swinging Beatles sound track. Almost everyone credited them with the new and buoyant spirit that seemed to seep into all phases of ordinary city life.

The Beatles sat comfortably on the fringe of the vibrant cultural revolution, having already contributed quite substantially to it. It went without saying that they had reinvented the music scene. Their clothes dominated teenage fashion with round-necked jackets and high-heeled boots. And they appeared daring thanks to their long, shaggy haircuts. "The Beatles changed everything," wrote a prominent English journalist. "Before them, all teenage life and, therefore, fashion existed in spasms; after them, it was an entity, a separate society."

Nothing was really settled by the fight, but according to Pete Best, "It was the beginning of the end of Stu as a Beatle." Stuart realized that the situation was hopeless. There was no place for him on that stage anymore. Paul had made that absolutely clear. And anyway, he'd had enough. He'd ignored his art for too long—he had barely touched a paintbrush in months—and he needed to reclaim that part of his life.

Later that week, he turned up at the Top Ten and told the others he was through with the band. It was all very matter-of-fact; there was no lingering resentment. In a magnanimous gesture, he even handed his bass over to Paul, who would go on to become perhaps the best rock 'n roll bass player ever.

With Stuart out of the picture, the Beatles could concentrate on more important matters. Music remained their top priority. Next on their agenda was making a record.

It was only a matter of time before word of their popularity spread to the music business. Bert Kaempfert, a popular German bandleader who also had a record label, invited the Beatles to be the backing band for an artist named Tony Sheridan, whom he was planning to record. The Beatles were stunned and overjoyed by the offer.

The session went so well that no more than two takes were required for any song. Convinced that the sound represented something new and unusual, everyone left the session feeling up-beat, no one more so than the Beatles. They regarded the session as their big break, the break that would lead to inevitable stardom. It didn't matter that the release was still a long way off or that the spotlight would fall on Tony Sheridan.

As it happened, however, the Beatles wouldn't be around for the record's release. A week after the session, their engagement at the Top Ten concluded, and like it or not, they were on their way back to Liverpool.

The Beatles always carefully groomed their image. Here they work on those iconic hair-dos before going onstage, 1964. © TERENCE SPENCER/CAMERA PRESS LONDON

Chapter 5

When the Beatles returned home in 1961, they were surprised to discover that the entire rock 'n roll scene had changed. Other bands, they learned, had bought into their renegade attitude. The music was loud, in-your-face loud, the stage presence disorderly and impolite. Anyone who disapproved could get stuffed, as far as the fans cared.

Without much ado, the Beatles took over their old starring role at the Cavern, where Bob Wooler relentlessly plugged their new single with Tony Sheridan, "My Bonnie." "Buy the record, folks," he'd implore between songs. "Make sure you ask for it at your favorite record shop."

In Liverpool, that meant NEMS—the North End Music Shop—which had a record department that was unmatched in its diverse selection, thanks to the exuberance of its demanding manager, Brian Epstein. Brian had little in common with the teenagers who infested his father's store like crows. Although he was only six years older than John Lennon, Brian was a *gentleman.* He wore immaculately tailored suits, spoke the King's English with a crisp, polished accent, and absolutely *hated* rock 'n roll. In fact, he loved serious music—theater, opera, and symphony—and lived for classical composers like Beethoven and Mozart. Even so, based on his efforts, "NEMS became the most important record outlet in Liverpool, if not in the whole north of England," according to a colleague. And because there was no local radio, if kids wanted to hear the latest rock 'n roll, they had to come to NEMS. For a teenager in Liverpool, NEMS was also the pipeline for reliable information. Someone hanging out there always knew what was going on. And if all else

Interior of a record shop, 1965. © Hulton-Deutsch Collection/CORBIS

failed, you could always go there and pick up a copy of *Mersey Beat*.

Mersey Beat was the brainchild of John's art school friend Bill Harry. A graphic artist with a passion for homemade magazines, Harry scrounged £50 from a friend and persuaded his girlfriend to leave her accounting job in order to crank out a magazine devoted to the music scene in Liverpool. From its first issue on July 6, 1961, *Mersey Beat* caught on with the local teenagers. Unfortunately, most newsstands and bookshops took only one or two copies to sell. It was an altogether different story at NEMS, however. Bill met with Brian Epstein and recalled that "straightaway, he agreed to take a dozen copies."

A week later, when Bill came to collect the money for those issues, Brian told him, "I can't understand it. They sold out in a day. Next time, I'll take *twelve* dozen copies."

The front page of the second edition was devoted to the breaking story BEATLES SIGN RECORDING CONTRACT! accompanied by one of Astrid's photos of the band. Eventually Brian got around to the question that would change everything. Sitting owl-eyed across from Bill Harry, he held up a copy of *Mersey*

Beat and wondered, "What about these Beatles?" He wanted to know everything: who they were, where they were from, what they sounded like, when they worked.

A month or two later, interrupting a routine inventory at NEMS, Brian confronted his colleague Alistair Taylor. "Do you remember a record by a band called the Beatles?" he asked out of the blue. Taylor had indeed. "My Bonnie" enjoyed terrific sales and was constantly on reorder. "They're playing at this place called the Cavern," Brian said. "We ought to go see them."

No one was more surprised than Alistair Taylor when Brian suggested they see the Beatles. "We both detested pop music," he recalled. "Even though we'd sold all those records [of "My Bonnie"], neither of us played it, nor particularly liked it." And Brian had no idea how to get to the Cavern, even though it was just two hundred yards from NEMS. When they got inside, they were shocked. "The place was packed and steam was rolling down the walls. The music was so loud we couldn't hear ourselves think. We were both in suits and ties, everyone was staring at us. We were very self-conscious."

Brian and Alistair took seats near the back and sat stiffly, with their arms folded across their chests. The Beatles, they thought, were shocking, disgraceful. "They could barely play," Alistair noted, "and they were deafening and *so* unprofessional—laughing with the girls, smoking onstage, and sipping from Cokes during their act. But *absolutely magic!* The vibe they generated was just unbelievable." Halfway through the set, Alistair glanced over at Brian and noticed they were both doing the same thing: tapping their hands on their legs.

Afterward, at lunch, both men sat puzzling over the experience. Brian asked Alistair for his opinion of the Beatles. Alistair thought they were "absolutely awful" but admitted there was something "remarkable" about them, something he couldn't quite put into words. Brian's reaction made Alistair uncomfortable. Smiling, Brian blurted out, "I think they're tremendous!" Then, out of nowhere, he grabbed Alistair by the arm and said, "Do you think I should manage them?"

Brian, according to Taylor, was "besotted" the minute he saw the Beatles. He couldn't stay away from them. At lunchtime, instead of joining his father and brother at a restaurant, as was customary, he would pull off his tie and head straight for the Cavern. He'd stand by himself at the back of the cellar, starry-eyed, entranced by the performance. Eventually, Brian invited the Beatles to his office in NEMS "for a chat," as he put it, and the band took him up on it.

"So, tell me," Brian asked casually, as they talked among the record stalls, "do you have a manager? It seems to me that with everything going on, someone ought to be looking after you."

The prospect of a well-connected manager fascinated the Beatles. John told his girlfriend, Cynthia, that "they were delighted that a proper businessman was actually interested in taking them on." John felt "the man from NEMS," as he called Brian, had "limitless influence." Cynthia could tell he had already made up his mind. So had the rest of the band. This was the chance they'd been waiting for. Their next meeting with Brian Epstein sealed the deal. John informed him that the Beatles were ready to accept his offer. "Right, then, Brian—manage us," he said.

By the end of 1961, riding the crest of local popularity, the Beatles, with Brian Epstein in their corner, were ready to take on the world.

· · · · ·

From the start, Brian made an effort to present the Beatles properly and "to smarten them up" for discriminating audiences. He insisted on some ground rules. From now on, eating onstage was out; so was smoking and punching one another, chatting up girls, taking requests, and sleeping. Lateness would no longer be tolerated, either. In addition, the Beatles were required to bow after each number, a big, choreographed bow, delivered crisply and on cue. And they had to wear suits! Leather and jeans were fine for the Cavern, Brian argued, but not if they wanted to be successful elsewhere.

Suits—never! John put his foot down. Black leather was one thing, but wearing business suits was going too far. Suits, he argued, went against everything rock 'n roll stood for. But Paul convinced him to give it a try. For the time being, at least. Later, they could always go back to their scruffy appearance.

Reluctantly, the Beatles agreed to follow Brian's rules. Convinced that they were on the right track, they saw only one barrier remaining between them and the possibility of real stardom: a recording contract with a major label—and it was so close, they believed, they could almost taste it.

Almost—but not quite. Throughout the beginning of 1962, Brian made numerous trips to London, playing a tape of the Beatles for anyone who would listen. At every record company, he promised that the band would be big—"bigger than Elvis!"—but the reaction was always negative: "They're nothing special." Or: "Groups with guitars are on the way out." Decca Records actually gave the Beatles an official audition, but they failed to stir enough enthusiasm. Afterward, in quick succession, the band was turned down by every other major British record label.

Brian Epstein in 1964, caught sitting alone and ignored at the Cavern, where he first discovered the Beatles.
© DAVID STEEN/CAMERA PRESS LONDON

All the rejections took their toll. Each time Brian returned empty-handed from London, the Beatles listened without grumbling, but their patience had worn thin. The Beatles felt they had done their share, reshaping their act to suit Brian's demands. They expected some results.

This also triggered some resentment within the Beatles. In the months since their return from Hamburg, a new star had emerged in the group. "Almost since he joined the band, Pete [Best] was the most popular Beatle," said Bill Harry, expressing a view shared by many early fans. "He was certainly the best looking among them, and the girls used to go bananas over him." Pete had immense stage presence. Unlike the other Beatles, who mugged shamelessly for the girls, Pete, unsmiling, ignored the crowd, which only heightened his mystique.

One can only imagine how much envy that stirred in Paul, who was sensitive to being upstaged. He'd already gotten bent out of shape by the way Stuart Sutcliffe had stolen the spotlight. Now suddenly Pete was crawling up his back. If this was allowed to continue, Pete would wind up as the Beatles' heartthrob. For the time being, however, Paul kept any resentment to himself.

On February 5, 1962, Pete called in sick a few hours before the band's gig at the Cavern. His timing couldn't have been worse. None of the other boys wanted to give up the gig. A few phone calls later, the Beatles determined that their buddies the Hurricanes happened to have a rare day off and were willing to loan out their drummer, Ringo Starr.

For Pete Best, it was the beginning of the end.

· · · · ·

On February 13, in a desperate last-ditch attempt to make good on a record contract, Brian doubled back to London for an interview with the only label that hadn't turned down the Beatles: Parlophone. Unfortunately, Parlophone was considered something of a joke in the recording industry. Its roster was dominated by insignificant acts: chamber music ensembles, light orchestras, Scottish dance bands, obscure music hall singers, and comedians. Hardly any pop bands succeeded on Parlophone, and those few that did soon ran out of steam.

The label's saving grace was its director, George Martin, a tall man, well over six feet, with thick, wavy, swept-back hair, liquid blue eyes, and an air of elegance that impressed everyone he met. He conducted himself with such dignity that every gesture seemed informed by graciousness and decency. Martin was also an accomplished musician, which gave him credibility with his artists. What he lacked, however, was legitimate pop artists—the kind of pop acts that now fueled every other record label. He was humiliated by the way Parlophone hadn't been able to get that together. "George was desperate to get something off the ground in the pop department," remembered his assistant, so when a friend called him about a promising group he'd heard, Martin agreed to a meeting with their manager, Brian Epstein.

After a first listen, Martin wasn't impressed. He considered the Beatles to be "a rather unpromising group." Even their original songs were "very mediocre," in his opinion. But he thought Paul's voice was rather enjoyable, and "a certain roughness" also pleased him. He decided there wasn't enough to go on, but instead of rejecting the band outright, he invited them to London, where he could meet them, hear them, and work with them in the studio.

In the meantime, the Beatles returned to Hamburg for a third extended appearance. They were eager to get away from Liverpool and thought it would be great to see old friends, especially Stuart and Astrid, who were planning to get married. Hamburg would also help take their minds off their sorry attempt to get a record deal. So they flew to Germany and charged through the airport, spotting Astrid Kirchherr in the terminal, waiting to greet them.

Ringo and John reminisce with Astrid Kirchherr en route from Munich before the Beatles' triumphant return to Hamburg in 1964. © MAX SCHELER/REDFERNS

"Where's Stu?" everyone wanted to know.

Her face was blank, still. Noting the blur of her gaze, John asked, "Oh, what's the matter?"

"Stuart died, John. He's gone."

The room went silent, out of focus. Paul, George, and Pete stumbled backward on their heels. John had been dealt a sideways blow. He didn't know how to cope with the news. His grief was numbing. Nothing registered. He gave voice to a single word: "How?"

Astrid was forthcoming with the details. Stuart, who had always suffered from severe headaches, began getting them with more intensity. They struck like electrical storms, sudden and scary, without warning. It was like "a bomb going off in his head," she explained. The headaches paralyzed him to the point of crippling agony. There had been spells when he couldn't see, couldn't think. And all Astrid could do was to sit there, stroking Stuart's hand or shoulder while he suffered wave after wave of pain. On April 10, a day before the Beatles left for Hamburg, Stuart collapsed and was convulsed with pain. Astrid's mother called an ambulance. It sped off to the hospital with Stuart inside, curled up in a ball, and it was there, pressed against Astrid, that Stuart died—of a brain aneurism or other disorder, it would never be certain.

The Beatles were stunned, confused. No one their age had died so tragically. They were still in their late teens. It was a real shock, es-

John photographed by Astrid Kirchherr, with the ghostly image of Stuart in the background, Hamburg, 1960. © Astrid Kerchherr/Redferns

pecially for John, who had looked up to Stu on so many levels. As a result, John began to drink, without regard for the consequences. It quickly got out of control, and his spring was filled with binges and brawls. Friends from Liverpool thought he'd gone "a little bit mad." But the drinking was a way to bury the pain of Stu's death. And part of it could be traced to frustration—frustration over the rejections, over the Beatles' smartened-up image, over their lack of a topflight drummer, over their indefinite future.

Their outlook brightened, however, when they received a telegram from Brian that Parlophone had agreed to a recording session with them. It was a stunning piece of news, a dream come true. By way of celebration, they clapped one another on the back and struck up a chant they often used to keep up their spirits.

"Where are we going, lads?" John would holler.

"To the toppermost, Johnny!" they responded.

"And where is that?"

"The toppermost of the poppermost!"

A recording session: the Beatles had dreamed of this for so long that it hardly seemed real. It was time to return to Liverpool, where they had become stars among the local teenagers. There was even an official fan club that reported their comings and goings. After all the hard work they had put in, it seemed as if things were starting to pay off.

John could hardly wait to tell his girlfriend, Cynthia, the good news. But when he arrived home and burst in with flowers and a smile, he could tell by the look on her face that something was wrong. Tearfully, Cynthia blurted out the news: she was pregnant. Frozen in place, he stared at her, dazed, unable to fire off a customary humorous remark. John's concern went straight to the Beatles. "I thought it would be good-bye to the group," he admitted later, when the shock had worn off. And just when it seemed as though a breakthrough was on the horizon. It appeared that fate had dealt him a blow—blowing it big-time. Still, he proposed they do the right thing and get married. There was no other way. That is how things were done in Liverpool, and John wasn't about to shirk his responsibility to Cynthia, marrying her on August 23, 1962.

The prospect of fatherhood made John increasingly resentful of the situation he was in, and he turned up the heat on an already smoldering relationship. Falling into black moods, he'd storm out of their flat, claiming to need cigarettes, and just disappear. Instead of blowing off steam and returning, he'd spend late evenings at the Jacaranda coffee bar or drinking at the Blue Angel.

That spring, friends often saw John wandering from club to club in the company of a spunky seventeen-year-old woman with jet-black hair to the middle of her back. According to reports, they'd been hanging out together, on and off, for a period of several months. Friends assumed he'd broken up with Cynthia, unaware that she was pregnant, let alone that she and John were married.

It had been hard keeping Cynthia hidden in the shadows. Brian Epstein had insisted that John keep his marriage a secret to avoid diminishing his popularity with the fans. "It was a calculated judgment on Brian's part that pop stars oughtn't to have partners," remembered a publicist for the Beatles. That was the thinking, at least, and apparently John was content to abide by it. Paul, consequently, broke up with his longtime girlfriend, Dot. Their success was all about freedom—freedom to pick and choose among the flock of available girls and freedom to live it up. With no wife to his credit—at least not in any published account—John could behave as most rock 'n roll stars did on the road. But it was an incredibly difficult time for John, who was still only twenty-one himself and completely unprepared for being a father.

Despite such upheaval, the Beatles kept their appointment with George Martin at Parlophone, only four days after they returned from Hamburg. They had to. This was the band's big chance, their only chance, and there was no way they could ignore it—not even if it meant leaving John's pregnant wife at home by herself. And even Cynthia somehow understood.

The session was held at Abbey Road studio, which was actually an old mansion in a sleepy suburb, St. John's Wood, in the north of London. It was an amazing place, and as the Beatles entered the building, Paul felt it was like "stepping into another world."

Though Abbey Road looked like any other house, inside, it was immense, actually a block of buildings that had been erected one behind the other, with corridors leading off at right angles to studios and offices. Lugging their equipment inside, the Beatles struggled to maintain their composure. It was awesome. And the *stillness* terrified them.

Studio Three, the corner suite, had been reserved for their audition. There was a feverish excitement in the air, and as they walked down the hall, the Beatles established a kind of frisky rapport, joking and firing off quick one-liners at one another to take the edge off their nerves. "We were nervous," Pete Best acknowledged. "We were feeling the old butterflies." Still, they threw up a smokescreen so as not to let on about their fears. "We were arrogant, cocky. *We're the Beatles!* We weren't about to let anything show."

All that changed, however, when they pushed through the doors to Studio Three. "Look at the size of this place!" they silently beamed to one another, thinking it resembled a football field. The room was wide and airy, with a faint hospital-like smell.

Abbey Road Studio

Located at the intersection of Abbey Road and Grove End in the sleepy London suburb of St. John's Wood, EMI Studios (always referred to as Abbey Road) wasn't meant to look like a recording complex. "It's a house!" the Beatles had groaned upon first setting eyes on it, and indeed it was, a former nine-bedroom Edwardian mansion set off by ample lawns, lilac hedges, and other neatly trimmed bushes.

Be that as it may, the Beatles were awed entering the building and "stepping into another world." Coming into Abbey Road for the first time, Paul recalled, "We thought, 'This is a small place,' but it just kept going on and on." The place was actually immense. Like a Chinese puzzle box, a block of buildings had been erected, one behind the other, in what was formerly the garden, with corridors leading off at right angles to studios and offices.

The Beatles were extremely nervous heading in there to record for the first time, in 1962. "We were feeling the old butterflies," recalled Pete Best, who was still their drummer at the time. Defensively, they clowned around so as not to let on about their fear. "We were arrogant, cocky. You know: *We're the Beatles.* We weren't about to let anything show."

Wires snaked along the floor, and there was a sound booth off to the side; otherwise it was empty. What a place!

The Beatles set up and ran through thirty-two songs that Brian had selected from their repertoire, barely stopping to catch a breath between numbers. They breezed through them all as though they were playing a lunchtime session at the Cavern, recording two songs cowritten by John and Paul: "Please Please Me" and "Love Me Do."

As an audition, the session brought mixed results. The Beatles handled themselves well in the studio, but they didn't impress George Martin or his colleagues at all. Martin enjoyed their voices, but the material troubled him. "They were rotten composers," Martin thought at the time. "Their own stuff wasn't any good." Also, he felt "the drummer was no good and needed to be changed." Pete had played well enough at their gigs in Hamburg and Liverpool, but when it came to making a professional sound in the studio, he was unable to pull it off.

George Martin, his assistant, and a sound engineer rather mercilessly critiqued the band. The harshness of their response surprised the Beatles, who listened, crestfallen, as the men laid into them for about an hour and were pretty forthright about their performance. They went over everything, from the lack of suitable material to improving their sound to their presence, which had somehow disappointed the record men. They got a real raking-over. When the final blow had been delivered, there was a long, anxious silence. Almost apologetically, George Martin asked the Beatles if there was anything *they* didn't like. After a well-timed beat, George Harrison answered, "I don't like your tie."

The Beatles in 1963, performing at an EMI reception launching their first album.
© PHILIP GOTLOP/CAMERA PRESS LONDON

The Beatles Fan Club

Even before the group's first recording session, the Beatles Fan Club had been organized. A teenager named Bobbie Brown, who followed the band from gig to gig, started it in 1961, sending out monthly chatty newsletters to local girls who paid the five-shilling dues and wrote in requesting intimate information about the lads: the color of their eyes and hair, their height, their ideal girl, car, and food, as well as their upcoming appearances. It was a small, passionate group at first, perhaps thirty-five or forty in all. But by mid-1962, the mail was descending on Brown's home in bulging sacks, and by the end of that year, the club had more than forty thousand members.

Beatles fans in New York on their arrival in August 1964. © Mirrorpix

The room went silent. For a split second, nobody breathed. Martin fixed George with a stern look, not certain what tack to take with the cheeky boy. Then he noticed a flicker of a smile at the corner of George's mouth. A joke! He'd been making a joke! What a perfect icebreaker. Martin's grin flashed approval ear to ear.

As the sound engineer recalled, "That was the turning point." The band clicked into Beatle mode, cutting up and peppering the technical staff with wordplay and double-talk in the manner of stand-up comedians. "During that one conversation, we realized they were something special." Martin and the others laughed so hard that tears soaked the collars of their shirts. "We've got to sign them for their wit," the engineer told Martin after the band had packed up. Martin promised to think about it, but he'd already made up his mind. The Beatles were a go.

He promised them that a proper recording session lay ahead. But first they decided to make some changes. The most important one concerned their drumming situation. They'd known all along that Pete Best was merely adequate, not nearly the musician for a professional rock 'n roll band. For months, the Beatles had had their eyes on the Hurricanes' drummer, Ringo Starr, and it was time, they decided, to pounce.

Ringo (whose real name was Richard Starkey) had what musicians called chops. He was an excellent drummer with a good feel. He was also very popular with other musicians because he wasn't a showboat; he played with a nice enough groove that served the songs without taking anything away from them. Plus, his ego never got in the way. Of all the drummers in Liverpool, bands ranked Ringo among the best. But he already had a gig with the Hurricanes, who were close friends of the Beatles.

What they didn't know was that Ringo had been looking for a better-paying job. He'd been toying with joining the Dominoes, another Liverpool rock 'n roll band, but John and Paul made him an offer he couldn't refuse: £25 a week, practically a king's ransom. They also waved around the prospect of a recording contract, which was a big deal to consider. The leader of the Hurricanes, who was disappointed but recognized a golden opportunity when he heard one, refused to stand in Ringo's way. "You should do it," he told his drummer. Whereupon Ringo promptly accepted.

The Beatles, who had sensed they were only one man away from being a great band, finally got what they'd always wanted: a world-class drummer.

Forevermore, the Beatles would be John, Paul, George, and Ringo.

Chapter 6

Ringo's joining the Beatles wasn't without bumps. The most violent reaction came from the band's fans, who were devoted to Pete Best. From the moment Ringo took the stage at his Cavern debut on August 19, 1962, he was greeted by an angry outcry. The crowd chanted, "Pete forever. Ringo—*never!*" Throughout the band's set, shouts punctuated the music: "Where's Pete?" *"Traitors!"* "We want Pete!" Afterward, when George stepped out of the band room into a dark, crowded passage, someone head-butted him under the eye, giving him a tremendous shiner.

Pete Best had his own wounds to tend to. He was crushed at having been sacked by the Beatles. It hit him suddenly and caught him seriously off guard. All that time he'd put in with the band, their would-be friendship, the dreams. Now, for this to happen—on the eve of a record deal. He considered it a "stab in the back." And the worst thing was the way in which he'd been dismissed. He'd gotten the news from Brian Epstein, their manager, in the office at NEMS.

"Pete," Brian told him, "I have some bad news for you. The boys want you out, and it's already been arranged that Ringo will join the band on Saturday." It was nothing more than a business decision, he assured Pete in as soothing a voice as was possible. "The lads don't want you in the group anymore."

The news knocked Pete sideways. Where were the Beatles? he wanted to know. Why hadn't they been men enough to tell him themselves?

Pete walked out of the office "in a state of shock." He'd kept his composure during those difficult minutes, but once he got home, he would admit, "I broke down and wept."

None of that deterred the Beatles. "Our career was on the line," Paul recalled, and the band knew how important it was to have a first-class drummer. Besides, it was evident they'd found their man from the moment Ringo took over the beat. Immediately they captured a spark that had eluded them for so long. The energy, the cleverness, the right groove—the *magic*—breezed into their overall sound.

In contrast to the other Beatles, who were middle- (John) or working-class (Paul and George), Ringo was "ordinary, poor," a hardship case. "He was not a barefoot, ragged child," recalled Marie Maguire Crawford, a neighbor who doubled as his surrogate sister, "but like all of the families who lived in the Dingle, he was part of an ongoing struggle to survive."

The Dingle, which was named by Irish immigrants after the arcadian glade in Ireland, bore little resemblance to its romantic namesake. One of the older inner-city districts in Liverpool, it was grim and really rough, the very edge of civilization, and housed the artisan working class—a mix of carpenters, plumbers, joiners, and others with a trade, who became as tightly intertwined as the project houses.

The Starkeys lived in an unusually roomy—Ringo recalled it as being "palatial"—three-bedroom house at 9 Madryn Street, a narrow alleyway lined with humble plane trees and squares of discolored, cracked pavement. Ringo's mother, Elsie, had been raised nearby, the youngest of fourteen children. She had learned that a woman should be self-sufficient, that independence meant getting a job, that spare time was devoted to the piano, and that evenings were for going out on the town.

Ringo—or Richard—was born on July 7, 1940. His birth was cause for much celebration on sleepy Madryn Street. Relatives stopped by at all hours to gaze upon the baby with the big, soulful eyes, who everyone agreed was the spitting image of his mum. He had his mother's long face and sensuous mouth, to say nothing of the thick, dark hair that would serve him handily twenty years hence. Ritchie, as he was called, bore hardly any resemblance to his father, who was quite a handsome man, with curly hair and a thin, narrow smile. He was Elsie's boy from head to toe, and she doted on him to the point of preoccupation.

Ringo's father was ill-prepared for fatherhood and even less willing to sacrifice for it, especially those wonderful nights on the town with Elsie. Within months after Ritchie's birth, things started to unravel for the Starkeys. Ringo's father withdrew further and further from the family. His nights on the town stretched into days. Often, he didn't even bother coming home from work, instead heading straight to a pub and then off somewhere crowded, wherever the action happened to be.

By 1943, the Starkeys' marriage was over. For his part, Ringo said he had "no real memories of Dad." He never made any effort to locate his father. Elsie was resourceful enough to pull through. She took a number of lowly jobs—scrubbing floors and doing laundry—until she dis-

No. 10 Admiral Grove, home of Ringo Starr. Dingle, Liverpool, 1964.
© Bettmann/CORBIS

covered her calling as a barmaid. Elsie, a gregarious woman by nature, enjoyed pubs and the people who came to them. There was a sense of community inside, and for the next twelve years she was a well-liked fixture in some of Liverpool's best pubs.

A few days before his seventh birthday, Ritchie complained about an upset stomach, and later sharp pains in his side. By bedtime, the pains persisted and his temperature had soared. His mother called for an ambulance and bundled him off to the hospital, where he had an appendectomy. In the aftermath, he developed peritonitis, a deadly inflammation of the abdomen, and lapsed into a coma. For three days, it was touch and go. Elsie was told to prepare for the worst. Ritchie was very lucky to survive. He underwent a six-month rehabilitation in a crowded hospital ward, then a relapse forced him back to bed, where he remained, barely mobile, for another six months.

Back at home, Ritchie found school a great and terrifying burden. So each morning, after wedging a stack of books under his arm and saying good-bye to his mother, he'd detour into the park and kill time until returning home. This made him something of an outcast in his neighborhood. Families in the Dingle may have been dirt-poor and largely uneducated, but they placed a serious emphasis on self-improvement.

Ringo at home with his mother, Elsie, and his stepfather, Harry, before the release of the Beatles' third album in 1964. © Max Scheler/K&K/Redferns

Until he was almost thirteen, Ringo was tutored by Marie Maguire. "He made incredible progress," she recalled, but then "he got sick again." It was a disastrous setback. This time it was tuberculosis, and it came as no surprise, considering the epidemic that raged through the filthy Dingle streets. This time, his mother wasted no time getting Ritchie to the hospital, where he remained—"the mayor of the ward," according to Marie—for almost a year.

The young patients were encouraged to join the hospital band. Ritchie played the drums, using "cotton bobbins to hit on the cabinet next to the bed." There was a natural feel to the way he held his hands, the impact of the wooden sticks on the wooden surface, and the patterns that emerged. He didn't just make noise; there was more to it than that, a complex range of sounds he could produce just by experimenting with his wrists. The more he played, the better he became, letting the energy take over.

Ritchie returned home in the fall of 1953, having "grown into a young man, but much frailer than other boys his age and somewhat disoriented." He'd fallen even further behind in school and was hopelessly lost in class. Ultimately, he left school, instead staying home and listening to music.

In 1953, his mother got married again, to a lovely man named Harry Graves. Much like Paul's father did with him, Harry helped introduce Ritchie to popular music and in 1957 bought him a secondhand set of drums for Christmas. The gift enthralled Ritchie—and changed his life.

Soon, he joined forces with a friend named Eddie Miles and formed a skiffle band, Eddie Clayton and the Clayton Squares, that played around the Dingle. But before too long, skiffle ran out of steam. Ritchie continued to play with Eddie but moonlighted with other bands as well, including Al Caldwell's Texans, who were desperate to have a drummer with his own kit. "When we told him we were going into rock 'n roll full tilt," recalled Johnny Byrne, the band's guitar player, "he said he was interested." With Ritchie keeping the beat, they played clubs in November 1958 as the Raging Texans and then as Rory Storm and the Hurricanes, which became one of the most popular bands in the city.

The Hurricanes, it seemed, were going places. Playing with them showed Ritchie that nothing—and no one—could compete with the thrill of the stage. But by 1962, Ringo, who got his nickname from the array of rings he wore, had grown dissatisfied. When the Beatles made their play, he hesitated only long enough to discuss their offer with a friend, who encouraged him to move on—and up—with a better band.

At last, after six years, stardom seemed possible for the Beatles.

• • • • •

The upheaval felt by Ringo's joining the band carried over into Abbey Road studio, where the Beatles were recording their first single, "Love Me Do." Something wasn't clicking. The song lacked drive. After listening to the tape, George Martin determined that Ringo was the problem. "He didn't have quite enough push," according to the engineer in the sound booth. The drums were too muddy, not as precise as the situation demanded. A week later, when the Beatles returned to the studio to redo the song, Ringo was stunned to learn that a session drummer had been hired to replace him. Despite the insult, he stepped aside, silently seething, and let the trained ears prevail.

The result was a success. The Beatles cut "Love Me Do," featuring a nifty harmonica riff by John, and its flip side, "P.S. I Love You," in a little under two hours. *Their first record!* The single flew out of the stores in Liverpool, especially NEMS, where they were already stars, but the rest of England gave it only a lukewarm response.

With hardly any time to catch their breath, the Beatles kept another appointment at Abbey Road on November 26, 1962, to undertake a follow-up. George Martin insisted they record "How Do You Do It," a catchy but lightweight tune

Fans trying to get into Liverpool town hall as crowds gather outside for a civic reception, 1964. © MirrorPix

by a professional songwriter, convinced it would be a hit. The Beatles, however, were dead set against it. "We just don't do this kind of song," they argued. "It's a different thing we're going for—something new." They wanted to record their own songs their own way.

Rock 'n roll bands as a rule *never* contradicted a producer. In the studio, the producer's word was law. But much to his credit, George Martin kept an open mind. Without hesitation, he allowed the Beatles to run through a Lennon and McCartney song, "Please Please Me," that he'd heard in an earlier, slower version. This time it really rocked, and Martin "knew right away" he had something special on his hands. "Please Please Me" was the world's real introduction to the Beatles, with catchy melodies, clever lyrics, seamless three-part harmonies, and dynamic instrumentation. It was as raw and rough edged as anything to come out of the British pop scene. And Ringo did away with any doubts that he couldn't handle the drumming, playing a precise, sharp backbeat that cuts loose at the end of the song with crisp bursts of percussion.

One can only imagine what George Martin felt when he listened to the playback. He was a serious musician, schooled in the formalities of symphony. "Please Please Me" really rocked. Martin knew it the moment he heard the tape. Grinning, he looked up over the console and exclaimed to the Beatles, "Gentlemen, you've just made your first number one record."

· · · · ·

Only six days after the release of the single, the Beatles appeared on a British TV show, *Thank Your Lucky Stars,* to plug "Please Please Me." The audience was completely unprepared for what they saw. Gliding across the screen were four extraordinary-looking boys, grinning at one another from beneath mops of outlandishly long hair and behaving like cuddly windup toys. No one had ever seen hair that long—or that shape—before. And their suits broke all the rules; they were smart and relaxed but also buttoned to the neck.

Once viewers got past the image, the music knocked them out cold. Hearing "Please Please Me" had the same effect as being thrown into an icy shower: the bracing rock 'n roll song chilled to the bone. The tone of it was powerful, unrelenting. *"Please pleeeease me, wo-yeah, like I please...,"* the Beatles sang, vibrating with uncommon energy.

A bomb had gone off. British rock 'n roll had arrived. "To those of us in England who lived for the next great American single," said journalist Ray Connolly, "it seemed like the Beatles were the promise we'd been waiting for all our lives." Up until that time, British rock 'n roll was basically American music copied—badly—by the British. Now the UK had an innovator of its own. "Please Please Me" hit the right groove, it was authentic, and it was entirely British.

Unlike "Love Me Do," which had to scrounge for airplay, "Please Please Me" dominated the BBC with the kind of all-out airplay that indicated a smash hit. The critics raved. And sales were strong, stronger than anything the record company had expected. Even in Liverpool, where the Beatles were already wildly popular, the impact was fantastic. Every time the band came into NEMS to see Brian, where he maintained an office, security measures had to be taken for their safety. Kids started coming around the shop, hoping to get a glimpse of the Beatles, blocking the doors so the ordinary customers couldn't get in. At one point, there were so many fans hanging around that Brian had to send the boys out the second-floor fire escape, onto the roof, where a ladder lowered them to safety.

Now everywhere the Beatles went there was an uproar. On a

The Beatles, posing in the backyard of one of their houses, 1964. © Terry O'Neill/Rex Features short tour through Britain with five other, bigger acts, the Beatles were last on the bill. But as the tour progressed, audiences began calling for the Beatles before the first act was finished. Singer Kenny Lynch, who introduced them, only had to put the microphone to his lips and say, "And now…" before he was drowned out by screams as the Beatles bounded onto the stage. "I think the Beatles shook those crowds up, even scared them a little," Lynch recalled. "They were so different, so tight, so confident, really playing their hearts out. It was like no experience those kids ever had before. Every girl thought they were singing straight to her; every boy saw himself standing in their place."

In fact, a group of young girls had already formed a fan club, which had come into full flower around the English provinces. It was like an exclusive sorority that teenagers—mostly girls—joined for five shillings dues, which entitled them to a chatty mimeographed newsletter and intimate information about "the lads": the color of their eyes and hair, their height, their ideal girl, car, and food (in that order), and also their upcoming appearances. At first, this was a small, passionate group, perhaps thirty or forty in number. But by mid-1963, the mail poured in in bulging sacks, demanding any speck of information about the fabulous Beatles.

"It all changed from that show," Paul recalled. "We took a break a day or two later, before the next leg of the tour, but when we went back out on the road, you could tell the whole balance had shifted, because all anyone wanted to hear was the Beatles."

"Please Please Me" shot to number five on the charts. Its success required the band to put out an entire album—ten songs, including "There's a Place" and "P.S. I Love You," all of which had to be recorded in a grueling daylong session. It didn't help matters that John was sick. He had developed a cold during the tour that was festering in his chest by the time the Beatles arrived in London, and his voice was shot. Still, the band managed to run through nine songs by dinnertime, most in only four or five takes. "They just put their heads down and played," recalled Brian.

One of the songs, entitled "17," was a breathless, all-out rocker that Paul and John had written one night on the way home from a gig. Its opening line—*"She was just seventeen, and she'd never been a beauty queen"*—had been bothering the boys for months. Something about it just didn't work. One afternoon in Liverpool, sitting on Paul's living-room floor, they came up with the solution: dropping the second part of the line in favor of *"You know what I mean."* That line—*"She was just seventeen, you know what I mean"*—eventually became the cornerstone of the album, certainly the heart of one of their most famous songs, which they retitled "I Saw Her Standing There." Nothing the Beatles had done so far packed more excitement into a number. From the opening bar, the song takes off, with all the spark and spirit of a rave-up. For two minutes and fifty-five seconds, the Beatles find the groove and don't let go.

At the end of the day, the Beatles were exhausted. Even so, they were still one song short. Wouldn't it be perfect, George Martin suggested, if they wrapped the whole project up that night? Despite their fatigue, the Beatles were willing, and they sorted through songs, looking for a killer finale. The engineer recalled that "someone suggested

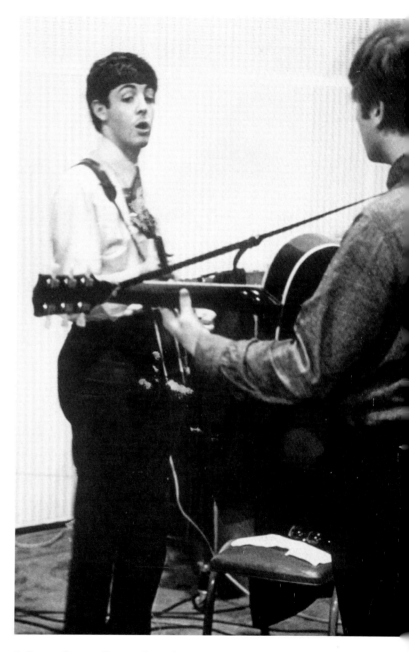

Before each recording session, John and Paul would preview their songs for producer George Martin. © Terry O'Neill/Rex Features

they do 'Twist and Shout,'" a staple of Beatles shows throughout the past year, but it required a tremendous vocal performance. It was John's song to sing. Was he up to it? No one, including John, was sure. He'd been straining his voice all day, draining it like a car running on fumes. There was enough left, he insisted, though admittedly his throat felt "like sandpaper" when he swallowed.

Everyone knew they'd have to get it on the first take, without a missed note or a recording glitch. There would be nothing left of John's voice after that.

The band returned to the studio and tuned up. It was cold in the room, and the air seemed thick and stale. John tore open a wax carton and gargled noisily with milk. He'd played most of the day in a rumpled suit, but sometime after dinner the jacket was removed and two fingers yanked down the tie. Now, without a word, he stripped off his shirt. He draped it over a bench, then walked to the microphone and nodded to the others: good to go.

It was obvious from the very first notes that John was straining for control. *"Shake it up, bay-be-eee..."* was more of a shriek than singing. There was nothing left of his voice; it was bone-dry. Between clamped jaws, contorting his face, he croaked, *"Twist and shout."* He had been struggling all day to hit notes, but this was different; this hurt. And it was painful to listen to. But the band rocked harder, building excitement with their energy, until the last tortured line, when Paul shouted, *"Hey!"*

John was wasted, near collapse, but the others already knew what he was about to find out: that "Twist and Shout" was a masterpiece—imperfect but still masterful, raw and explosive. In the control booth, there was jubilation as George Martin and his crew knew they had "got it in one" take.

The Beatles had their first album, but there was still no time to rest. For the next ten days, from February 12 to 22, 1963, they hopscotched around England, playing one-nighters on a crazy zigzag route. It was a brutal grind, and they grumbled—grumbled mightily. But after the grumbling came the work. Exhausted though the Beatles may have been, they never passed up an opportunity to promote themselves. Drive all night to a gig, shake

Beatles fans screaming outside the Palladium as they await the arrival of their idols, October 1963. © MIRRORPIX

hands with a record seller, sign autographs at a record shop, play a dance, a talent show, they did everything–*everything*–necessary to get their name around, to win fans, to succeed. There was a feeling shared among the band that if they kept at it, the dream would come true.

The record deal was rewarding, and it had kept them going for quite a long time. But it was nothing compared with the news Brian delivered the following week, while the Beatles played a club near their home. "Please Please Me" had not only hit the charts, it eventually shot to number one in England.

· · · · ·

For the Beatles, everything changed with their leap to the top of the charts. Once their record hit number one, their popularity extended far beyond the Cavern walls and far beyond the Mersey banks, establishing them as something of a national phenomenon. When they rejoined the five-act tour, everywhere the Beatles played, earsplitting screams broke out at the mere mention of their name. The minute the lights went down, the crowd went crazy. And after each act finished its set, the theaters shook with kids hollering,

Paul and Jane Asher in 1965, during the early days of their courtship. © Mirrorpix

"We want the Beatles! We want the Beatles!"

By the end of 1963, the Beatles and their manager had grown weary of dragging themselves back and forth between Liverpool and London, sometimes two or three times a week. Besides, none of the boys had a place of his own. One might say they still lived with their parents, but even that was inexact. Interaction with families and friends was becoming awkward. Besides, all of the Beatles except George had steady girlfriends, with whom they were spending steady time. And with the constant invasion of fans, as Ringo noted, "it was impossible to go home." Even John, whose wife, Cynthia, and son, Julian, born on April 8, 1963, remained Merseyside, lived more or less out of a suitcase.

As a remedy, Brian rented the Beatles an unfurnished apartment in London, to use as a base when they were in the city on business or playing nearby. The little flat was frightfully sparse—no furniture to speak of, just three bedrooms with nothing more than single beds and lamps. A tortured stereo in one corner played a never-ending selection of loud music. But if there was a bleakness about it, Ringo and George, at least, didn't seem to mind. As George recalled, "It was such a buzz because we'd been brought up in little houses in Liverpool, and now to have a posh apartment in Mayfair, and with a bathroom each, it was great."

A crash pad was all right for George and Ringo, but John, for one, had a family to think about. Eventually he moved with Cynthia and Julian into a tiny fifth-floor apartment nearby. Paul, too, decided to split from the group's place. He'd become involved with a scarlet-haired teenage actress named Jane Asher, who was a familiar face on British TV and on the stage. More and more, after a hectic day conducting Beatles business, Paul would make a beeline for her family's town house. Throughout the fall of 1963, Paul and Jane spun madly from the West End to Covent Garden to the National Theater to various clubs, to anywhere there was something of cultural interest going on. Plays, exhibitions, concerts, parties, one after another—there was never a dull moment.

Friends described Jane Asher as "your typical girl next door." She was all of seventeen when Paul first met her and already a fixture in the London acting community. She was slim-waisted, small, and striking, with delicate features and a pale, creamy complexion. After an adolescence of auditions and finishing school, Jane developed enormous poise accentuated by a lithe theatricality. Like Paul, Jane had the aura. "She was smart and sexy," said one of Brian Epstein's assistants, "one of the most charming young women I ever met."

Paul immediately fell in love with her, as well as with her family. In November, Jane suggested that he move permanently into the Ashers' magnificent town house; if he liked, the attic room was available, along with honorary membership in the family. The magnanimity of it must have shocked Paul, who had been living out of a suitcase—or in a filthy van—for so long that it was hard for him to remember the last time he had his own room. To say nothing of a girlfriend who was living only one floor below. It was not an invitation that required much deliberation. "For a young guy who likes his home comforts," he noted, it was a dream come true.

But it was only part of the dream. With all the hoopla, Brian Epstein suggested the Beatles take their show to America. The Beatles had always regarded the States as the promised land—home of their early singing idols Chuck Berry, Buddy Holly, Little Richard, the Everly Brothers, and, of course, Elvis Presley—but their records weren't being released there. Capitol Records, which had the rights to Parlophone for America, frankly refused to put out British pop records. According to Capitol's top executives, the Beatles were "nothing," and they turned the group down cold. A New York lawyer sent copies of "Love Me Do" and "Please Please Me" to all of the other major American record labels and came up empty-handed. Only a tiny independent Chicago label called Vee-Jay heard the magic and agreed to put the two singles out in a few months' time.

Meanwhile, the Beatles launched their next single in England, "From Me to You," which came crashing onto the charts at the number six position and sold 200,000 copies in the first week alone. A British writer observed, "By now the Beatle legend was beginning to grow. It was becoming clear they were something rather special." That was putting it mildly. All of London, it seemed, had their name on its lips: *the Beatles!*

Unfazed by the attention, the band plowed through appearances on television and in theaters, promoting "From Me to You" without pause. And everywhere they went, fans greeted them with screams that lasted right through their act.

Following the taping of a TV show, the Beatles were invited to hear a new rhythm and blues band that was playing in a club just outside of London. The Beatles had been hearing a buzz about the band for some time, and when they got to the club, it turned out to be a tumultuous scene. The place was mobbed with a wild and woolly bunch of fans who shouted and screamed and danced on tables. The Beatles heard right away what a "great sound" the band was making. The two guitar players—Keith Richards and Brian Jones—"just had presence," according to Ringo, who summed up their appeal with one word: "Wow!" Mick Jagger, the band's vocalist, seemed more than stylish. And everyone loved the band's name: the Rolling Stones.

Later that night, as the two bands talked until dawn, none of the musicians could have dreamed of the incredible fame that awaited them or the cultural upheaval brewing in Britain. But there were already signs of a musical revolution. Besides the Beatles and eventually the Stones, inroads were being made by groups like the Yardbirds (with a guitar player named Eric Clapton), the Pretty Things (whose singer was Rod Stewart), and

Lead singer and founding member of the Rolling Stones, Mick Jagger, with Keith Richards and Bill Wyman, 1960s. © MIRRORPIX

many others. But it was the Beatles, everyone agreed, who set the British music scene on fire. The fan mail was the best evidence of what lay ahead. Complete strangers wrote to thank the Beatles for their music and to pledge undying loyalty to the band. Thousands of letters poured in every week—bundles, cartons, sacks of mail, including autograph requests, love letters, stuffed animals, and pictures. And their fan club had grown to forty thousand members in England alone.

To satisfy their fans, George Martin begged the Beatles for another hit record. A song they'd begun writing after a gig seemed as if it might fit the bill. Paul had sketched out a lyric that showed promise. The way Paul saw it, he'd sing, *"She loves you,"* and the band would respond, *"Yeah...yeah...yeah."* John liked it, though he thought the answering business was a "crummy idea." They set to work, whipping out their guitars, and in a few hours' time had the bones of a song in place. George Martin listened to a rundown of it in the studio and thought it was

YEAH! **YEAH! YEAH!**

"brilliant…one of the most vital songs the Beatles had written so far."

What the Beatles built into the song provided a perfect, lasting image for them: the *yeah-yeah-yeah*s and the falsetto *ooooo*s (when performing this, they shook their heads in unison, setting off rapturous shrieks from the fans) became enduring symbols. Nothing identifies them more vividly.

Unlike the band's previous records, "She Loves You" touched off a nationwide reaction the press immediately called "Beatles fever." Before the record was even released, Parlophone had orders for a staggering 235,000 copies. No act in memory had spurred such demand. "We were like kings of the jungle then," John remembered.

Unfortunately, that wasn't the case in America. No one in the States knew who the Beatles were. Vee-Jay had released their first two singles, but even by Paul's account, they were "a flop." American disc jockeys ignored them completely. Brian Epstein, their manager, went to New York in an attempt to get things started, but not a glimmer of interest in the Beatles surfaced anywhere he went.

All that, however, was about to change. On Sunday, October 13, 1963, the Beatles were scheduled to appear on a British television show called *Sunday Night at the London Palladium*. Practically every TV set in the country was tuned to it each Sunday night as the top English and visiting American performers took part in the prestigious variety show. In Ringo's estimation, "There was nothing bigger in the world than making it to the Palladium."

Fans had begun gathering outside the theater just after the Beatles' arrival for a rehearsal. By late afternoon, the situation outside the stage door intensified. There were a hundred or so kids

Police holding back crowds of fans waiting to see the Beatles, July 1964. © MIRRORPIX

hanging out there—more than the Beatles could safely deal with. Later, as the band left the theater and headed to their car, hordes of fans converged from everywhere and it all happened at once. An incredible roar went up, not merely any roar but an earsplitting blast of excitement, mixed with surprise and awe. Pandemonium broke out on the sidewalk. Pushing and shoving started as the Beatles ran through grabby hands, diving for cover into the car. In ten minutes, every newspaper had been alerted to the story.

BEATLEMANIA! screamed the front page of the *Daily Mirror*. Headlines didn't come any more eye-catching than that. Every paper carried photographs of a dark street scene, with a line of police struggling to hold off a mob of screaming girls. Where earlier there had been two hundred fans outside the Palladium, by show's end there were two thousand. According to eyewitnesses, "Screaming girls launched themselves against the police—sending helmets flying and constables reeling."

During the next few weeks, it was the same everywhere the Beatles went. Stampeding fans battled for tickets to their shows and crashed through police lines. Girls fainted. Reporters demanded interviews. There seemed no limit to the wild scenes.

BEATLEMANIA! When the boys returned from a weeklong tour of Sweden, thousands of screaming fans crowded Heathrow Airport to greet them. By coincidence, the com-

motion caught the attention of American TV host Ed Sullivan, who was arriving in London to scout talent for future shows. Intrigued, he cornered a few giggling fans and asked if they knew whether a celebrity was arriving. Was it a member of the royal family? he demanded. The girls just laughed and sashayed away. After an airport official told him it was the Beatles, Sullivan wrote down the name and instructed his producer to find out what he could about them.

It didn't take Ed Sullivan long to learn that a phenomenon called the Beatles was streaking through all of England. He wanted to scoop them up exclusively for America, before his competition got wind of them. That meant striking a quick deal with Brian Epstein. Wisely, the Beatles had refused to consider an American visit until they had a hit record in the States. But Brian Epstein had an instinct—a good instinct—that the time was right. Besides, Ed Sullivan's show in America was as popular as *Sunday Night at the London Palladium* was in England. It would be the perfect US showcase for the Beatles.

Some American label just *had* to put their records out properly. To avoid an embarrassing situation, the head of Parlophone's parent company flew to the States and told Capitol Records, "You *must* do it." Capitol was surprised by the ultimatum. The

Marsha Albert's Gift to the Beatles

In mid-November 1963, a teenager named Marsha Albert was so intrigued by reports about the Beatles coming from England that she wrote a letter to her local deejay, at WWDC in Washington, DC, asking to hear something by the band. No one at the station had ever heard of them. But a disc jockey named Carroll James hunted down an import copy of "I Want to Hold Your Hand" and invited Marsha Albert to introduce it on the air.

On December 17, Marsha read a few lines of copy that James had scrawled on the back of a traffic report, then launched the Beatles onto the American airwaves for the first time ever. When the song was over, James invited the audience to pass on their opinion of it. As he recalled it, "The switchboard just totally went wild." Every line lit up. He continued programming the song every night that week all the way through Christmas. As far as the Beatles were concerned, it was the best gift they could have asked for that holiday season—thanks to Marsha Albert.

Brian Epstein (standing, center) surrounded by his budding NEMS roster: the Beatles, Gerry and the Pacemakers, and Billy J. Kramer with the Dakotas, 1964. © MIRRORPIX

The Beatles pose in front of the Stars and Stripes, promoting their first American tour, which started in February 1964. © MIRRORPIX

company had already turned down the Beatles plenty of times. Now it was being forced to put them out.

Fortunately, this time Capitol was handed a lulu of a record that launched the Beatles—and the label—into the stratosphere. The record Brian gave them was "I Want to Hold Your Hand," the Beatles' most inspired song yet. It was part joyous rocker, part roller-coaster ride, and it came at the listener from every angle. No doubt about it, "I Want to Hold Your Hand" was like no record anyone at Capitol had ever heard before. If they were forced to re-lease the Beatles, then this was a record they could get behind.

While Capitol dawdled, Parlophone released the Beatles' second album, *With the Beatles,* in England. Even the NEMS store in Liverpool was unprepared for the runaway demand. "I'd never seen anything like it," recalled the man who managed NEMS in Brian's absence. "There were hundreds of kids trying to get into the store. Police showed up to keep things under control. Our cashiers were so overwhelmed that everyone, myself included, worked the counter until the store closed." In fact, all over Great Britain, teenagers mobbed record stores to get their hands on copies of *With the Beatles.* On that first day alone, an astounding 530,000 copies of the album were sold, along with another 200,000 more singles of "She Loves You."

Finally, America took notice. In mid-November 1963, all three US television networks sent film crews to England to report on Beatlemania. An American teenager who saw them on TV wrote a letter to her local disc jockey asking to hear something by the Beatles. After he played "I Want to Hold Your Hand"—the first time the band was played on any American station—every telephone line lit up. So he played it again the next hour and the next, then played it every night that week, which sounded an alarm at Capitol Records.

With all the airplay, Capitol decided to move up the American release of "I Want to Hold Your Hand" to December 27. It would not arrive in time for Christmas, but the Beatles didn't care.

At long last, they were going to America.

Chapter 7

The Beatles were nervous en route to America — nervous about all the reporters accompanying them on the plane, nervous about what they'd find in New York, nervous about their chances with American audiences. During the long flight on February 7, 1964, John sat rigidly behind the others, holding Cynthia's hand and staring at the back of the seat in front of him. All he could focus on was not being embarrassed. What if they arrived and no one knew who they were? Even the usually confident Paul was relaying to a fellow passenger his own misgivings, when he was interrupted by word from the cockpit. As he remembered it: "The pilot had rang ahead and said, 'Tell the boys there's a big crowd waiting for them.'"

As the plane taxied toward the gate at Kennedy Airport in New York City, the Beatles scrambled over one another to get a better view of the scene unfolding outside at the terminal. Everywhere they looked it was wall-to-wall kids. Shouts—whoops and cheers—erupted inside the plane. Close to three thousand American fans had been gathering there since early morning, spurred on by New York's most famous radio deejays broadcasting live from the airport. The Beatles were beside themselves with joy. As they stood by the aircraft door, grinning and gaping at the crowd, a radio commentator breathlessly struggled to describe the scene. "No one," he said, "I mean *no one,* has ever seen or even remotely suspected anything like this before!"

But that was only the warm-up. During a hastily arranged press conference at the airport, the hard-core New York reporters got a dose of Beatles magic.

"Will you sing for us?" a reporter shouted over the racket.

"No!" all four Beatles replied in unison.

"We need money first," John shot back, sending snickers through the crowd.

"What about you, Ringo? What do you think of Beethoven?"

"I love him," Ringo said. "Especially his poems."

"Are you for real?"

"Come and have a feel."

Afterward, due to the large crowds, the Beatles were forced to escape. As it was reported in the newspaper, "The Beatles were lifted bodily by two policemen each, and each young man was placed…in his own Cadillac limousine." A handful of girls actually threw themselves at the cars, then the Beatles sped off toward the city. "It was like a dream," Paul recalled. "The greatest fantasy ever."

But the fantasy didn't end there. Outside the Plaza Hotel, where the Beatles shared a fabulous ten-room suite during their stay, hundreds of fans gathered, causing gridlock. A throng of girls clogged the street and swarmed over the fountain and tiny statue in the arcade on Fifth Avenue. Police held them back as best they could, but it grew hard as the day grew long. The hotel doors had to be secured; fans who got inside were soon ejected. Exhausted from the flight, the Beatles camped out on the hotel sofa, watching themselves on television and listening to music.

Unlike in England, where there was only one radio station, New York had dozens of them, which amazed the Beatles no end. All those songs they had been dying to hear by their American music heroes were right there within earshot. And American deejays, they discovered, took requests. "We phoned every radio station in town," John explained, "saying, 'Will you play the Ronettes'" or Marvin Gaye or Smokey Robinson or the Shirelles? They stayed up all night, talking to deejays and listening to the radio.

The next morning, George came down with a flu, and when his temperature nudged past 102, he was ordered to bed. A friend had to stand in for him at rehearsals for *The Ed Sullivan Show.*

The Beatles took New York by storm in February 1964, initiated by their rousing press conference moments after arriving at JFK Airport. © MirrorpiX

The other Beatles went sightseeing in New York and fell in love with the city—while New York fell in love with the Beatles. They posed for photographers in Central Park, then took an impromptu tour of Harlem. Record shops beckoned from every corner. The three boys pressed their faces against the car windows, staring at the fabulous scenery. There were more places they wanted to visit, but because of all the fans, they had to stay locked in their suite. As one friend later described it, "The Beatles were really like prisoners."

It was almost a relief to get down to work. On Sunday afternoon, just before *The Ed Sullivan Show* broadcast, the Beatles arrived at the television studio, along with George, who was still feeling nauseous and unsteady. The boys got comfortable backstage. A stack of telegrams lay on a ledge by the mirror. One, marked URGENT, caught Paul's attention, and as he read it his face corkscrewed into a mad grin.

It said: CONGRATULATIONS ON YOUR APPEARANCE ON THE ED SULLIVAN SHOW AND YOUR VISIT TO AMERICA. WE HOPE YOUR ENGAGEMENT WILL BE A SUCCESSFUL ONE AND YOUR VISIT PLEASANT. GIVE OUR BEST TO ED SULLIVAN. Paul looked up beaming: "Signed, Elvis."

115

John, in a customary display of wit, shot back, "Elvis who?" The show itself went off beautifully. Ed Sullivan was a big, stiff man with very little personality, who sauntered onto the stage to introduce the acts. "Now, yesterday and today our theater's been jammed with newsmen and press from all over the world," he said, "and these veterans agree with me that the city's never witnessed the excitement stirred by these youngsters from Liverpool who call themselves the Beatles." As he said their name, screams rippled through the audience. "Ladies and gentlemen—*the Beatles!*"

Few viewers had known what to expect. Until that moment, all that most Americans had really seen of the Beatles was scattered newspaper photographs. A Beatles performance was something else entirely, and the power of it, the charge they sent through the audience, moved teenagers in ways they'd never been moved before. For starters, there was that boyish charm, which the Beatles (especially Paul) had perfected. Hearts melted in an instant when the boys looked directly at the camera and projected those gorgeous smiles.

What's more, rock 'n roll bands didn't usually perform on television. And when they did, in most cases they lip-synched to their records. Therefore, seeing the Beatles playing live was a fairly eye-opening experience. And how those boys could play! As they hit the *ooooo*s during "She Loves You," Paul and John exaggerated the shake of

The Beatles with Ed Sullivan for *The Ed Sullivan Show* in New York, February 1964. © Mirrorpix

their long-haired heads, which triggered shrieks of delirium from the new fans. Later, they played "I Saw Her Standing There" and "I Want to Hold Your Hand," thrilling the crowd.

Girls especially were caught up in the performance. During the last song, viewers at home were given a special introduction to the band, with the name of each Beatle superimposed over a lingering close-up; John came last, and below his name was an unexpected postscript: "Sorry girls, he's married"—at last a formal acknowledgment of the Beatles' heartthrob status.

The cat was out of the bag. Until now, Brian had demanded that the Beatles keep Cynthia a secret from the press, fearing that fans, especially teenage girls, would lose interest if they knew John was married. Rules had been established: she was never to be mentioned by the lads, nor could she come to the Beatles' performances, which angered Cynthia and John. Fans had always been fascinated by the rumor that one of the Beatles had a wife; now it was a relief to John that everybody knew. Meanwhile, it would

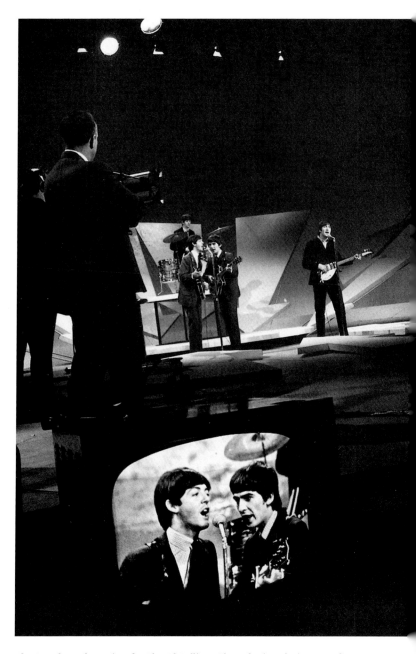

The Beatles rehearsing for *The Ed Sullivan Show* during their tour of the USA, February 1964. © MIRRORPIX

Clowning with Cassius Clay, whom they met in Miami, following their performance on *The Ed Sullivan Show*. © CURTIS/CAMERA PRESS LONDON

be safe to say that American girls didn't lose a drop of interest. John was still securely in their hearts.

It was estimated that 74 million viewers tuned in to watch the Beatles' US television debut—a record for America. But over breakfast the next morning, with newspapers spread across the table, the Beatles were disappointed by the tone of the reviews. They were called "a fad" and even "a nightmare." One magazine said, "Their lyrics (punctuated by nutty shouts of yeah, yeah, yeah!) are a catastrophe."

If the negative reviews bothered the Beatles, they refused to let it show. "If everybody really liked us, it would be a bore," John said during a press conference that lasted almost three hours. The Beatles, for their part, never lost their poise. When someone asked about the review that said they couldn't carry a tune, John said, "We're gonna see a doctor about that." The Beatles seemed able to handle anything thrown at them, and they were delighted when the president of Capitol Records stepped forward to present them with two gold records.

Everywhere they went, it was the same. In Washington, DC, huge crowds—a mob scene—greeted them at the train station. And the Washington Coliseum was the biggest place they'd ever played, a crusty old 18,000-seat arena that catered to ice hockey and boxing matches. Brian hadn't quite prepared them for the size of the place, or mentioned that they'd be performing on a platform in the middle of the crowd. But, again, it was love at first sight between the Beatles and their fans. The audience of mostly teenagers went berserk when the boys appeared; the crowd jumped to its feet, screaming uncontrollably in a sustained roar that lasted through the band's twenty-eight-minute set.

Afterward, the Beatles were dizzy from exhaustion—and exhilaration. Ringo, especially, was over the moon about the fans. "They could have ripped me apart and I wouldn't have cared," he cried backstage. "What an audience! I could have played for them all night."

If that weren't enough, the Beatles continued their American visit by playing two sold-out shows at New York's prestigious Carnegie Hall, where, until that night, no rock 'n roll band had ever set foot. Then they appeared on another *Ed Sullivan Show,* broadcast live from Miami, which drew the largest TV audience in history. While in Florida, they sparred with the celebrated young boxer Cassius Clay, who would eventually change his name to Muhammad Ali.

In all, the Beatles accomplished what their British forefathers had been unable to do: they conquered America and came home to England as heroes.

· · · · ·

Two days after returning to London, the Beatles headed back into Abbey Road studio to work on songs for a new album. They could hardly wait to get started. Since the beginning of the year, they had barely played a note that wasn't drowned out by screams, and as

A Mob at Penn Station

On February 12, 1964, there was the usual mob scene at Pennsylvania Station when the Beatles' train arrived back in New York from Washington, DC. Thousands of fans jammed the upper waiting area, with the overflow milling through the lower concourse and scattered along the platforms. In no time, it became a perilous scene. The transit police force was unprepared to handle such an enormous crowd and panicked when a mad rush of teenagers broke through a line of barricades to greet the arriving train.

Unbeknownst to the fans, however, the Beatles' car had been detached from the train and diverted to an isolated platform at the opposite end of the station, where security guards planned to evacuate the boys by a private elevator. But some resourceful kids had already anticipated that, and in the end the boys merely charged up the stairs and jumped into a taxi idling on Seventh Avenue.

musicians, they had become frustrated. John and Paul had written steadily over the past few months and had a ton of songs to choose from. A version of "Can't Buy Me Love" had been recorded earlier, but they quickly laid down the tracks for "You Can't Do That," "And I Love Her," "I Should Have Known Better," "Tell Me Why," and "If I Fell." John and Paul usually switched off singing the lead vocals, but they also wrote "I'm Happy Just to Dance with You" for George to sing.

The Beatles were delighted to be recording again, but they were also about to become movie stars. While they were in America, Brian had negotiated a deal for them to star in their first full-length film, a comedy, which was being written especially to showcase their wacky personalities. The boys seemed perfectly comfortable performing music onstage, but no one—especially the Beatles—knew if they could act. It was a gamble from the start, but, as the movie's producer recalled after the first day on the set, "The Beatles fell right into it; they were naturals."

The work itself was more demanding than they'd expected. For one thing, they had to report for costumes and makeup at six o'clock in the morning, which meant getting up at five. The Beatles were used to sleeping until noon, so it took everything they had to make it to the set on time. And learning their lines was an uphill battle. Instead of memorizing the script, they made it up as they went along. According to another actor in the movie, "You never knew what they were going to say or do." But somehow it all came together wonderfully. The Beatles were *funny.* They were naturals in front of the camera. The only thing missing was a good title for the picture.

Everyone had been referring to the film as *"The Beatles Movie"* until something more suitable came along. Despite lots of good effort, however, no one could come up with something that sounded as if it belonged on a theater marquee. There are several versions of how the title was finally arrived at. What they all agree on is that it occurred during a lunch break at the movie studio. Paul and George were talking about how Ringo abused the English language, saying things seriously that came out funny. They called

The Beatles on location for *A Hard Day's Night,* March 1964. © Mirrorpix

them "Ringoisms." One in particular always made them laugh. Following a late-night performance, they explained, Ringo had sighed and said he'd "had a hard day's night that day." When the movie's producer heard that, he clapped his hands and said, "We've just got our title!" And from that moment on, their movie was called *A Hard Day's Night.*

Of course, that meant John and Paul had to write a song to go with the title. They were swamped with work, acting and recording, but the next morning, only ten hours after the producer had requested it, they'd already completed the task, writing what became one

The gang celebrating Paul's birthday: Arthur Kelly with a date (left), Gerry Marsden (middle), George Harrison and Pattie Boyd (right). © MIRRORPIX

of their most famous songs. "A Hard Day's Night" was recorded the next day, on April 16, 1964, and from the extraordinary opening chord, it was evident that the Beatles had raised the bar for all pop songwriting. The energy the song delivers is explosive, full of fireworks, and musically it was as daring as anything they'd ever done.

During the filming, George became infatuated with one of the extras in the film, a beautiful young model named Pattie Boyd whose face was well-known because of a famous television ad for potato chips. She had been cast in the movie, along with her younger sister, Jenny, as a way of dressing up the scenery around the Beatles. According to friends, Pattie not only had an eye on George on the set, she had been following his career from a distance since the start. George picked up the signals on the very first day of production, during a scene in which Pattie appeared as an immodest schoolgirl. "When we started filming, I could feel George looking at me," she recalled, "and I was a bit embarrassed." It might have been less awkward had she not been "semi-engaged" to a boyfriend with whom she'd been living for two years. At the time, the boyfriend said he felt "confident about [his] relationship with her," but within a week, Pattie and George were making their own plans.

It was easy to understand George's attraction to her. Pattie was an angelic-looking young woman, pleasant and unpretentious, with a style that was as natural as it was alluring. In a genuine, matter-of-fact way, she seemed to be a reference point for all the new fashion that was percolating in London: chic and funky clothes, shaggy haircut, sexy miniskirt, pale makeup, antique jewelry. "Whenever fashions changed, Pattie was in there first with all the right gear, looking beautiful as ever," Cynthia Lennon wrote in one of her memoirs. She always managed to look fabulous with very little effort, and George fell in love with her because of her beauty, style, and easygoing personality.

In those days, it was taboo for the press to publish a picture of one of the Beatles with his wife or girlfriend. The band's private lives were strictly off-limits. But once Pattie came on the scene, all bets were off. A reporter for the *Daily Mirror,* one of London's leading papers, got wind that John and George were about to fly off on a weekend holiday, one of them *with a new girlfriend* in tow, and the newspaper was determined to break the story. Reporters eager to identify the young woman swarmed the hotel, looking for the two couples. It got so bad, they became prisoners in their rooms. "In the end, Cyn and I had to dress as maids," Pattie recalled. "They took us out a back way, put us in a laundry basket, and we were driven to the airport in a laundry van."

Somehow, Ringo's steady girlfriend, Maureen Cox, was spared. For a long time, she remained in Liverpool, where she worked as a hairdresser. Although she spent a lot of time visiting Ringo's Montagu Street flat in London, the press, as of yet, had not caught on.

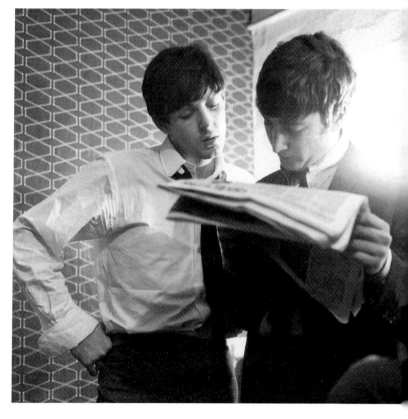

Paul and John backstage at East Ham in 1963, perusing reviews of their shows. The Beatles avidly read all press reports of their exploits.
© Jane Bown/Camera press London

YEAH! YEAH! YEAH!

It seemed as though everyone in London followed the Beatles like a favorite soap opera. Not a day went by that didn't offer ample stories about their adventures, even if they were only rumor and gossip. Papers reported on where they were last seen and with whom, how they were dressed, what they had for dinner, and when they went home (and with whom). The gloves had come off; the Beatles' private lives were now considered fair game.

After the band wrapped up work on the movie and new album, they left for a tour of Scandinavia, following it by leapfrogging several continents, then zooming through New Zealand and Australia. Wherever they went, they were welcomed like heroes. Their arrival in Amsterdam was greeted by an elaborate motorcycle escort that wound through the city, flanked by units of police and the civil guard. Afterward, the Beatles took a glass-topped boat for a ten-mile trip through the Amstel Canal. "We passed at least 100,000 cheering people who lined the streets on each side to wave, and sometimes almost touch, the Beatles as they passed," wrote a reporter who accompanied them. Fans leaped from canal bridges as the boat passed underneath.

Every city, every situation, brought out people who wanted to touch the Beatles. And the fans—everywhere the Beatles went, fans expected, *demanded,* some sort of personal response: sign this, wave, say hello, touch me, kiss me. They stopped at nothing: invading the Beatles' hotel suites, throwing themselves in front of their cars, jumping from balconies, following Cynthia and the other musicians' girlfriends. It never let up. In Australia, it really got crazy. When the Beatles landed in Adelaide, they were loaded into a convertible and paraded along a nine-mile stretch of highway

Police holding back crowds of fans waiting to see the Beatles, July 1964. © Mirrorpix

Fans at the ABC Theatre as the Beatles arrive. © Mirrorpix

lined by 250,000 people, nearly half the city's population. An additional 30,000 fans crammed into the square outside the gates of Adelaide's Town Hall, where the Beatles were awarded the key to the city. The same thing occurred in Melbourne, where another 250,000 people lined the route from the airport to the Beatles' hotel.

Occasionally, the situation became dangerous. Things turned very scary when Ringo's car was surrounded by 3,000 fans, many pressing up against the windows, pounding on the doors, and screaming. A police officer built like a bulldozer slung Ringo over his shoulder and made a beeline for the hotel, but he stumbled. In a flash, they went down. Ringo was knocked to the ground and engulfed by the crowd. By the time he was rescued, he was scuffed and badly shaken. Later that same afternoon, 20,000 people stood outside the band's hotel, chanting, *We want the Beatles!* while 4,000 policemen held them back. It was "frightening, chaotic, and rather inhuman," according to a trooper on horseback.

What was going on? the Beatles wondered. How had things gotten so out of hand? And if this was how things were in Australia, what would America be like when they returned there later in the year? In America, Beatles fever was running at an all-time high. Public demand was incredible. In Chicago, 18,000 tickets were sold before a single ad appeared for their concert. The entire block of 12,000 tickets for Philadelphia were sold in seventy hectic minutes. For all of the upcoming twenty-seven US concerts, the same thing: sold out, sold out, sold out.

The Beatles arrived back home in London determined to figure out how things had spun out of control—but first they had a date at the movies.

· · · · ·

The premiere of *A Hard Day's Night,* on July 6, 1964, wasn't normal, even by movie-gala standards. By 7:30, an hour before the premiere was to begin, the streets around Piccadilly Circus, in London, were jammed by a crowd of twelve thousand fans struggling to get a glimpse of the shaggy-haired stars. Inside the London Pavilion, the Beatles, dressed in stiffly pressed tuxedoes, stood with their families and the posh crowd. Joining them were Princess Margaret and the Earl of Snowden. Earlier that day, the band had watched a run-through of the film at a private screening with Brian and the producer, who insisted they "behaved like delighted little kids" watching themselves romp across the screen. Slouched down in the orchestra section, with their feet up on the backs of the seats in front of them, they wolfed down popcorn and howled like hyenas or groaned with embarrassment, depending on the scene. The producer, watching from the balcony, was confident they had a hit on their hands.

With few exceptions, the critics agreed that *A Hard Day's Night* was a winner. In the usually stiff-lipped *New York Times,* the newspaper's movie critic praised it as "a whale of a comedy" that "had so much good humor going for it that it is awfully hard to resist." Elsewhere, critics called it "offbeat" and "delightfully loony." Even John said,

127

"I dug *A Hard Day's Night.* We knew it was better than other rock movies, though not as good as James Bond."

The fans obviously agreed with him. The next morning, when the movie officially opened, there were lines around the block at theaters all over that continued every day for months.

It was the perfect time, the Beatles agreed, to revisit America.

· · · · ·

The lure of America had once involved a fear of the unknown, but when the Beatles returned on August 18, 1964, there were no surprises. Their records were, according to a midwestern newspaper, "on jukeboxes in a hundred thousand joints and drugstores." Capitol Records had flooded the market with an unprecedented 2 million copies of their brand-new album, and airplay was nonstop. Meanwhile, *A Hard Day's Night* flickered across five hundred screens. Everywhere the Beatles went, crowds amassed in staggering numbers: three thousand, eight thousand, fifteen thousand, twenty thousand, *more.* "America was now very aware of the Beatles," said their road manager, Neil Aspinall, "and things were crazy."

Crazy: it was a word occurring with disturbing frequency in describing the shifting American scene. There was a feeling in the United States that the peace of the 1950s was in rocky disarray. Young people were struggling—often chaotically—to find a means of self-expression. The civil rights movement, galvanized by Martin Luther King Jr., was attempting to dismantle segregation and change the way people lived with one another. The threat of nuclear war aroused greater interest in pacifism. And changing attitudes toward sexuality jump-started a debate concerning public values and private moral choices.

Everything seemed connected to a growing disenchantment with the establishment and was set to a soundtrack by the Beatles. The boys served as hip role models for a restless generation of Americans grappling with questions of individual freedom and expression.

Fans wearing Beatles dresses as they wait for the group at the film premiere of *A Hard Day's Night* at the London Palladium, July 1964. © MIRRORPIX

Their hair, especially, disturbed adults. According to a journalist, "It was perceived to be threatening the very fabric of American society. And it was intolerable."

Crazy, indeed. Amid all the blind spots surrounding these issues, the Beatles were a visible target. Parents blamed them for contributing to teenage delinquency. There was no precedent for the kind of mayhem the Beatles provoked. In Los Angeles, a police lieutenant covering the Beatles' arrival said, "It scares you. It's just beyond me. I've *never* seen anything like this."

The scene was the same everywhere. Crowds of kids, mobs of them, screaming and fainting, battling through police lines to touch their beloved Beatles. As for the shows themselves, lasting a scant thirty-one minutes, they were like sitting inside a funnel cloud. The four Beatles would rush onstage unannounced, clutching their instruments like body armor while flashbulbs exploded around them in a hail of blinding light. Most of the kids continued screaming throughout the entire performance. A solid wall of earsplitting sound shook the seats, rumbling through the darkness, wave after wave of it. "It felt like an earthquake," re-

The classic stage routine, with the entire sound output coming from those puny amps. © MIRRORPIX

called an astonished eyewitness who would remember the experience for the rest of his life. "It would start at one end of the arena and continue to the other. It was incredible to do nothing but stand there, letting it wash right over you."

The Beatles needed relief from the mobs. In most cities, they went straight from the performance to the airport and headed to the next stop on the tour as a way of avoiding the crazy crowd scenes. For convenience and safety, they chartered their own plane. It made road life easier for the Beatles, not having to be pestered by fans and autograph seekers.

The concerts were a different matter. At the concerts, the Beatles left themselves vulnerable to the crowds. "It was pretty scary just about everywhere we went," recalled a journalist who never strayed far from the Beatles' side. In New York, at Forest Hills Tennis Stadium, dozens of fans stormed the stage, and at one point Ringo was knocked off his stool by an overenthusiastic girl who had leaped over a line of police kneeling in front of the stage. In Cleveland, as soon as the Beatles hit the stage, jelly beans, toys, and much heavier objects were launched at their heads. And in Boston, a fight broke out that stopped the show.

Fortunately, in Los Angeles, the atmosphere grew calmer. The Beatles played to a worshipful crowd of nineteen thousand people at the Hollywood Bowl, the gorgeous open-air amphitheater at the foot of the Hollywood Hills. Behind them, reaching into the spectacular starlit sky, another ten or fifteen thousand fans were massed in the woodlands. "Welcome to you in the trees!" John shouted, as the other Beatles swung around to look, taking in the human scenery. Everyone was well-behaved. For a change, John recalled, the Beatles could actually *hear* what they were playing, which made the show a highlight of the tour.

The next day, at a garden party thrown by Capitol Records, it seemed as if every movie star turned up to greet the Beatles. If the Beatles were starstruck, they didn't show it. Longtime movie fans, they enjoyed meeting their screen heroes. Even Elvis's manager arrived in a station wagon loaded with presents for the boys.

The American tour dragged on through most of September. The cities sped by in a blur: Denver, Cincinnati, New York, Atlantic City, Philadelphia, Indianapolis, Milwaukee, Chicago, Detroit. Everywhere they went there were greater displays of mayhem, the fans ever more determined to cross the Beatles' path. The boys had banked a record $1 million from the tour, which seemed amazing considering it wasn't that long ago that they'd been making $20 a gig. Now, with three gold records and a hit movie to their credit, a newspaper put the Beatles' earnings at roughly $56 million.

· · · · ·

Through it all, John and Paul continued writing songs. Once they returned home, Paul would drive out to John's new house, where they would spread out in a little attic room overlooking the garden to "kick things around" for two or three hours. Occasionally, when Paul was tired, he arranged to be driven out to John's in order to spend the travel time relaxing or reading the newspaper. One day, just as the limo was turning into the driveway,

Where's Ringo?

A shock wave shuddered through Copenhagen Airport on June 4, 1964, as the Beatles' plane approached the runway. More than two thousand kids had been waiting since dawn for their heroes to arrive, and as the plane taxied toward the terminal, a deafening roar went up. All hell broke loose on the ground as the cabin door popped open and out bounded the Beatles: John, Paul, George—and Jimmy.

Paul, John, and George, with Jimmy Nicol, June 1964.
© Bettmann/CORBIS

There had been no time to inform the crowd that Ringo wasn't aboard. Only a day earlier, he'd collapsed during a stressful photo session. His throat had been especially sore, but it wasn't until he was rushed to the hospital that he learned he had laryngitis and would need to have his tonsils out.

Instead of canceling their upcoming tour, Brian Epstein convinced the Beatles to replace Ringo with a session drummer. Jimmy Nicol, who was twenty-four, not only had great hands, he happened to fit the part as well, with a round, cherubic face, a wicked sense of humor, and long hair like the Beatles. Somehow, Jimmy took it all in stride. "He played well," Paul said with customary graciousness. But a few days later, when Ringo showed up feeling refreshed and recharged, the Beatles were thankful to have their old mate back behind the drums.

Paul put down his newspaper and asked the chauffeur how he'd been. "Oh, working hard," the man replied, "working eight days a week." Bells went off in Paul's head. *Eight days a week!* "It was like a little blessing from the gods," he recalled. No sooner had John answered the door than Paul dropped this phrase into his hands. They practically dashed upstairs and began spitting out lyrics, just "filling it in from the title," as Paul remembered. Bam, bam, bam.

They also wrote "No Reply" and "I Feel Fine," both of which would appear on the Beatles' next album. While they were recording "I Feel Fine," a happy accident occurred. They had finished a decent take of the song and were about to listen to the playback. "We were just about to walk away," Paul remembered, "when John leaned his guitar against the amp." The closeness of the guitar and amp produced an electrical spike that sent distortion echoing through the studio. For the Beatles, discovering feedback was like hitting the lottery. No one had ever considered using a sound effect like that before. "Can we have that on the record?" Paul asked George Martin. No problem. They re-created the accident, and each time seemed to get more control over the sound.

In a year, the Beatles would almost single-handedly reinvent the way music was recorded, but for now they were happy to revel in their discovery. It was a completely new and exciting experience. In the fall of 1965, they put it all together. Like everything else they'd done, their unique sound was the result of exploring the past and using early pop music influences to go their own way. As John described it, "We finally took over the studio."

Chapter 8

The whole of London now moved to the beat of the swinging Beatles soundtrack. Almost everyone credited them with the new and enchanting spirit that now seemed to be seeping into all aspects of city life. There was a revolution in the arts that could be seen on the walls of London's galleries. Similarly, rock 'n roll had taken over the airwaves, with bands like the Animals, the Kinks, the Yardbirds, Herman's Hermits, the Dave Clark Five, the Who, and of course the Rolling Stones. Fashion had been transformed by designers whose boutiques turned a seedy lane in Soho called Carnaby Street into a high-style mall. As one shopper recalled, "There were so many different things you could wear—red corduroy trousers, green corduroy trousers, flowery shirts, polka dots every-where. Before that, all we had were gray and brown."

It went without saying that the Beatles rejuvenated, if not reinvented, the local scene. Their music spoke directly to young people and eloquently expressed teenage feelings. Their round-necked jackets and high-heeled boots dominated fashion. And they appeared daring thanks to the cut of their hair. According to a famous British journalist, "The Beatles changed everything."

But the Beatles weren't interested in social upheaval. They wanted to make records, not waves. And despite the success of *A Hard Day's Night,* they had no great desire to become movie stars. Their second film, *Help!,* made in 1965, was more work than fun. They'd begun experimenting with pot, which didn't help matters. The Beatles were so stoned, so distracted filming the movie that they couldn't remember their lines. As a result, it seemed to take forever to complete their scenes.

Bob Dylan, 1964. © MIRRORPIX

Their adventure with marijuana began when they were in New York and met Bob Dylan, whom all of the Beatles idolized. Dylan was a pop god, as far as the Beatles were concerned. Paul had discovered him first, buying *The Freewheelin' Bob Dylan* album before they left for a tour of Paris at the beginning of the year. That record hit the turntable the moment the Beatles settled into their hotel suite. "And for the rest of our three weeks in Paris, we didn't stop playing it," John recalled. Considering he was only a twenty-year-old folk singer, the way Dylan wrote and sang—the strong intelligence, the unusual phrasing—did a major number on the Beatles. "Vocally and poetically, Dylan was a huge influence," according to Paul.

When Dylan caught up with the Beatles in New York, they were ready for anything. Dylan was eccentric and intense but cool, very cool, in a way that only another pop act could appreciate. Even so, when he suggested they smoke marijuana, the Beatles were stunned—and a bit stupefied.

They were also uncomfortable, having never smoked pot before. But the boys found its effect spectacular—"We were just legless, aching from laughter," George told a friend—and extremely liberating. Or so they thought. For the moment, it seemed like fun, but it would ultimately cause problems as, hopelessly stoned, they tried to look and act straight with friends and family.

It didn't seem to hurt, however, when it came to their music. *Help!* needed a soundtrack album, so John and Paul got down to business, doing what they did best—writing songs. They worked furiously, high on pot and adrenaline, jotting ideas on pages that they ripped from spiral-bound tablets when they grew dissatisfied. Almost every line of every verse of every song was reworked several times. They spit words out quickly, sometimes talking over each other, testing rhymes and inflections in the process. Things occasionally got lost in the flow, but that had always been the way they worked best. "We made a game of it," Paul recalled. "John and I wrote songs within two or three hours—our 'time allotted.' It hardly ever took much longer than that." Or else they lost interest and moved on.

Almost immediately, they cranked out a treasure trove of new and unique songs. "Ticket to Ride," which was released as a single in advance of the movie, sounded like nothing a rock 'n roll band had ever produced. "We sat down and worked on that song for a full three-hour songwriting session," Paul recalled, "and at the end of it we had all the words, we had the harmonies, and we had all the little bits." Aside from "Help!" and "Ticket to Ride," the other gems were "You're Going to Lose That Girl," "It's Only Love," "You've Got to Hide Your Love Away," and "I Need You."

Two weeks before filming started, Ringo took a day off in London and married his girlfriend, Maureen Cox, making him the second of the Beatles to tie the knot. "He's the marrying kind," John explained after the news hit the papers, "a sort of family man," which was true enough. Only a few months earlier, Ringo had told a reporter, "I want to get married someday and I don't plan to wait too long about it."

YEAH! **YEAH! YEAH!**

Both George and Paul also had steady girlfriends; George continued to date model Pattie Boyd, whom he had met on the set of *A Hard Day's Night,* and Paul was still dating Jane Asher, the up-and-coming actress who had already appeared in a popular TV series and was performing regularly in the theater.

The Beatles spent the first half of 1965 ping-ponging between the movie studio and the recording studio. Aside from a brief vacation abroad, all their spare time was filled with radio and TV appearances to plug their latest album. It seemed as if their lives were bogged down in work, without much freedom. Then, in early May, Brian Epstein showed up on the movie set and assembled the Beatles in a dressing room. He acted "rather secretively," according to Paul, who sensed that something extraordinary was about to happen. "I've got some news for you," Brian announced with great theatricality. "The prime minister and the queen have awarded you an MBE."

None of the boys had any idea what he was talking about. An MBE might have been a sports car, for all they knew. (George later joked that it stood for "*Mr. Brian Epstein.*") As mostly working-class lads from Liverpool, they had little knowledge of the titles given to upper-class Britons. What they discovered was that under a charter signed in 1917, the king and his successors were empowered to recognize distinguished service to the Crown through honorary awards. The highest rank was Knight or Dame, the lowest was Member of the Most Excellent Order of the British Empire, or MBE. Usually it was awarded for acts of heroism in war. Giving it to pop stars was unprecedented. The Beatles were astonished.

The Beatles displaying their MBE medals at a press conference in 1965. John later returned his medal. © Peter Mitchell/Camera Press (G/S) London

Brian Epstein and George Martin at Abbey Road studio. © Mɪʀʀᴏʀᴘɪx

They thought they were unworthy of the honor. So, too, did many of the war heroes who had already been awarded an MBE. One man decorated for bravery fired off an angry letter to Buckingham Palace, saying, "I am so disgusted with the Beatles being given this award that I am considering sending mine back." Another complained that giving the award to the Beatles made "its meaning seem…worthless." Discussing it among themselves, the Beatles decided not to accept the award, but Brian convinced them otherwise.

In the midst of all the MBE ruckus, the Beatles continued to record, laying down the tracks for some of their most famous songs: "I've Just Seen a Face," "It's Only Love," and "I'm Down." During one long session, Paul was eager to try something new. He dragged a stool to the middle of the studio and, with the lights dimmed, played guitar to a ballad he had just written, which would become the most recorded song of all time.

"Yesterday" had been rattling around Paul's head for nearly two years, since he "woke up one morning with the tune," tumbled out of bed, and even before washing his face ran through it at the upright piano in his room. Had it come to him in a dream, as he initially suspected? Was it something he'd heard that he refused to let go of? Paul hadn't the foggiest. The chords just kept coming, one after another, falling neatly into place. The melody sounded familiar, like one of the old standards his father used to pound out on the piano after dinner, and though the overall impression it left was "very nice" indeed, Paul convinced himself that the tune was something he'd stolen. Still, the melody haunted him. "It was fairly mystical," he explained. He couldn't let go of it.

Friends assured him that the tune was original—all his. A songwriting acquaintance insisted he was "onto something important." Even so, Paul remained unconvinced. He felt it was something he'd heard before. But everywhere he turned, the trail went cold. No one recognized it; it didn't even resemble another song.

One night, while he was playing the melody on a friend's piano, her mother swept through the room, wondering if "anyone wanted some scrambled eggs." Without missing a beat, Paul improvised a lyric for his new tune: "Scrambled eggs...oh my, baby, how I love your legs..." The words fit perfectly. Too perfectly, in fact, because for more than a year he was unable to shake those awful lines.

"Scrambled Eggs," as he now called the song, became Paul's burden. Every day, every week, for a year and a half—without fail—he tinkered with it, trying to come up with good words. Rhyme schemes were tested and discarded in search of a word or two that would give the song its identity. Usually, Paul could rattle off lyrics in his sleep, but it was no use—the right phrase, the

"Michelle...Ma Belle"

One day in 1965, John reminded Paul about "that French thing" he used to play at parties in Liverpool. Paul knew exactly what he was talking about: a precious, "rather French-sounding" instrumental he'd spun using a fingerpicking technique. "Well, that's a good tune. You should do something with it."

Coincidentally, Paul had been tinkering with a lyric built around the name Michelle and thought it might match up with the melody. To give it the musical lilt the name seemed to suggest, he decided to weave in a few French phrases as an accent. "Michelle...ma belle." It so happened he was spending the weekend with his old Liverpool schoolmate Ivan Vaughan, whose wife taught French at a primary school. At Paul's urging, she helped fill in the rest of the French expressions. By the time Paul played it for John, the song was pretty much fleshed out but still lacked a chorus. "I had been listening to [the old song] 'I Put a Spell on You,'" John recalled. "There was a line in it that went: 'I love *you*, I love *you*, I love *you*.'" Changing the emphasis to *love*, he "added a little bluesy edge" to the song, and they'd finished another one.

one that would unlock the song, eluded him. He and John had put songs aside before and come back to them, but this one was different. Paul knew the melody was exquisite. Frustrated, he ran it by John, who thought the song was "lovely" but had nothing to offer.

In May 1965, Paul left for a two-week vacation to Portugal with Jane, ready to abandon the song forever. But the minute his plane touched down, the words began to flow. During the five-hour drive from the airport to the beach, Paul ran through "Scrambled Eggs," picking it apart. The stumbling blocks began to give way. "I remember mulling over the tune," he said, "and suddenly getting these little one-word openings to the verse." *Da-da-da...yesterday...suddenly...fun-il-ly...mer-il-ly...* No sooner did he have that foundation than the rhymes began to connect and blend. "'Yesterday'—that's good," he decided. "'All my troubles seemed so far away.'"

The song was *exactly* right by the time he returned to London. "What about having a string arrangement?" George Martin asked Paul when they were ready to record it. Paul cringed, worried that it might sound too syrupy. That wasn't at all his style, but he agreed to at least try a string quartet.

They spent an afternoon mapping it out, devising cello and violin lines to complement the melody. Actually, arranging it wasn't that tough. "Yesterday" lent itself beautifully to the silky sound of strings, and the two men—Paul humming parts, with George Martin writing down the notes—created the gorgeous accompaniment that underscores the record. The entire session took less than three hours to complete. Forty years later, the song is still the most played record of all time.

• • • • •

The Beatles had undergone quite a change since they first appeared on the pop scene. Outwardly, they remained the same lovable mop tops, their smiles as familiar and flashy as the grille on a Jaguar, their extreme hairdos as symbolic as the queen's crown. Privately, however, they were changing. Their use of drugs had become more frequent. The generation gap was widening, and with it came a heavier feeling that they could no longer play the charming but cheeky lads.

Part of it was because of the maturing music scene. One night in May, the Beatles crept into a darkened box at the Albert Hall in London to catch Bob Dylan's performance, and they left speechless, in awe. He seemed so intense, so emotionally *out there,* expressing himself so eloquently. How did he manage to do that—to write and sing so beautifully and from such a remarkable place?

John and George found part of the answer quite by accident one night at a dinner party organized by a British dentist. A strange group of guests was assembled, and the two Beatles, with Cynthia and Pattie, were uneasy from the moment they walked through the door. Nothing out of the ordinary occurred until after dinner, when they prepared to leave. The host pulled John aside and talked to him seriously in a corner of the room.

"We've had LSD," John revealed to George in a bone-dry voice. The drug, a powerful and dangerous substance that caused mind-altering hallucinations, had been slipped into their coffee. "I didn't really know what it was," George remembered, "and we didn't know we were taking it." So little was known about LSD, in fact, that it wasn't even illegal at the time. It meant nothing to George, but John was furious. He had not come to dinner to have drugs put into his coffee.

George celebrates his twenty-first birthday with a fat stogie, piles of mail, and a comely fan. © MIRRORPIX

Daily Mirror

Dragnet out for Roy...

ALEX G... SWOOP—TWO SE...

Sir Alec finds it rough ...ing..

By MIRROR REPORTER

DRAMATIC swoops were made yesterday by Scotland Yard detectives investigating the £6,000 jewel robbery at Princess Alexandra's home.

MPs may unite to get ban on sta...

Mumbling good-byes, they grabbed Cynthia and Pattie and sped off toward a nightclub in London. For a few minutes everything was fine. "Suddenly I felt the most incredible feeling come over me," George remembered. John felt it, too. They saw streaks of blazing light behind their eyelids. The tone of their bodies felt different. It was scary. They quickly left the nightclub and went out onto the street. Pattie was feeling agitated and out of control. Later, she threatened to break a store window until George dragged her away. "We didn't know what was going on and thought we were going crackers," John explained. "It was insane going around London on it."

The bizarre hallucinations continued until dawn. Objects took on a weird fun-house distortion. At one point, they imagined flames shooting up into an elevator in which they were riding. Said John, "We were all screaming, *'aaaaaaagh,'* all hot and hysterical."

But if the LSD was scary and dangerous, it also allowed the Beatles to look inside themselves. The drug, they decided later, possessed an undeniable power—a spiritual power—that made a lightbulb go on in their heads and gave them a kind of enlightenment. But in July 1965, after their first unwitting trip, John and George were too shook up by the experience to experiment with LSD. "There was too much to sort out," George said, too much of an emotional upheaval.

In fact, they were exhausted—exhausted from all the exposure. The Beatles were everywhere at once—in magazines and newspapers, on television, in the movies, on the radio. "You couldn't walk down the street without having us staring at you," John said. Everyone wanted a piece of the Beatles: promoters, celebrities, dig-

John and Paul reading the *Daily Mirror.* © MIRRORPIX

nitaries, even the queen. Early in July, after looking over their schedule, Brian announced to the press that contrary to the group's usual practice, the Beatles would not be doing any TV or radio appearances to promote their new record. They were going to take a breather—just not yet. It would come *after* another American tour.

· · · · ·

No sooner had the Beatles touched down in New York than the shift in the scene was evident. Music was everywhere; it seemed to have taken over the streets. They not only heard the new groove on the radio but could see it in the styles as well as the manner in which the kids carried themselves. The airwaves were awash in records by pop groups like the Byrds, Sonny and Cher, the Turtles, the Dixie Cups, and of course Bob Dylan.

Sonny and Cher. © Mirrorpix

The Byrds (from left to right): Roger McGuinn, Kevin Kelley, Gram Parsons, and Chris Hillman. © Mirrorpix

Gone was the innocence that had accompanied the previous two tours. There was no official greeting at the airport, no prearranged waving to the fans; despite a heavy turnout at Kennedy Airport, the boys remained completely out of sight throughout the arrival process. Even at the usual press conference, the Beatles showed none of their trademark wit. And at the hotel, the Beatles remained locked in their suite practically the entire time they were in New York.

Part of the reason for this was security. The Beatles were always in danger of being trampled by fans. But another part was self-preservation. The obligations heaped on the Beatles were extraordinary. More than ever, they had no idea what they were getting themselves into.

The work in New York placed even greater demands on the boys. On Saturday, August 14, they taped their third appearance on *The Ed Sullivan Show.* "Four hours of constant rehearsals," according to one observer in the theater. "Six songs, no break, just total dedication." Afterward, as the sun went down, the Beatles boarded a helicopter bound for Shea Stadium, in Queens. It was a clear, beautiful night, but the Beatles were gaunt faced and anxious, barely glancing at the scenery. Between the helicopter ride, which they dreaded, and the destination, which seemed unreal, it was all they could do to keep their food down.

A 56,000-seat horseshoe where the Mets played baseball, Shea Stadium was bathed in a halo of light and looked like a stage prop from eight thousand feet up. "For the boys," recalled their press officer, "seeing the stadium was an absolute high. They were awestruck, *gobsmacked,* as the Liverpool expression goes." No band had ever played to an audience so large. The show was already in progress as they flew overhead. The pilot switched on a two-way radio so his passengers could monitor the sound onstage. As he swung above the parking lot, a deejay shouted over the stadium PA system, "You hear that up there? Listen…*it's the Beatles!* They're *here!*" The sky lit up as thousands of flashbulbs exploded. "It was terrifying at first when we saw the crowds," said George, "but I don't think I ever felt so exhilarated in my life!"

Beatles fans scream at the top of their lungs during a concert at Shea Stadium, August 15, 1965. © BETTMANN/CORBIS

It was too dangerous to land the helicopter on the baseball field, so it was diverted to a strip near the old World's Fair site, where the Beatles were transferred into armored cars. "It was organized like a military operation," recalled a photographer who was along for the ride.

As the Beatles scanned the stands from the Mets' dugout, they fell back in laughter. Everywhere they looked were kids—wall-to-wall kids. "It seemed like millions of people," Paul recalled, "but we were ready for it."

As the Beatles charged from the dugout to the stage situated over second base, more than fifty thousand kids jumped to their feet and screamed, wept, and thrashed in what must have sounded like pure bedlam. A reporter compared the roar to "a dozen jets taking off." The Rolling Stones' lead singer, Mick Jagger, who was watching from a seat behind the first-base dugout, was visibly shaken by the crowd's behavior. "It's frightening," he told a companion.

More than fifty 100-watt amplifiers had been set up along the base paths of the diamond, but they were no match for the wall of sound from the stands. The fans drowned out all the singing and most of the music. "It was ridiculous," John remarked of the experience. "We couldn't hear ourselves sing." During two numbers, he wasn't even sure what key they were in. And later, when watching the replay on TV, he noted, "George and I aren't even bothering to play half the chords, and we were just messing about."

For promoters everywhere, however, the Shea Stadium concert was a major breakthrough. Forevermore, it turned a pop music performance into an event.

The Beatles tour continued across North America, rekindling the excitement in Toronto, Atlanta, Houston, Chicago, and Minneapolis. In each city, the usual concert halls had been rejected in favor of open-air stadiums and arenas, with screaming and hysterics a part of every show. In Los Angeles, with a few days off, they got a real treat: an invitation to visit with Elvis Presley, whom they had all idolized as kids.

Perhaps more than anyone else, John was shaken by the experience of meeting his boyhood idol. He acted foolish, clowning and jabbering, when he was introduced to Elvis. The other Beatles were speechless. No one knew what to do or say. After a brief, embarrassing silence, Elvis summoned them to sit down beside him but grew weary of the Beatles' vacant stares. "If you guys are just gonna sit there and stare at me, I'm goin' to bed," Elvis huffed. "I didn't mean for this to be like the subjects calling on the King. I just thought we'd sit and talk about music and jam a little."

"That'd be great," Paul said, suggesting a few songs they could play together. Unwinding gradually, they tore through a few of Elvis's hits, including "Blue Suede Shoes," with Elvis singing and Paul playing the piano, before finishing with the Beatles' "I Feel Fine." Still, it was an awkward evening, one they would be reluctant to repeat. Even at this point the Beatles could learn one of life's important lessons: that sometimes it is better to live with your fantasies than to make them come true.

• • • • •

George with Pattie Boyd on the set of *A Hard Day's Night.* © K&K ULF KRUGER OHG/REDFERNS

After the Beatles' final performance, in San Francisco, everyone was ready to head home. The pitch of the crowd in San Francisco was a bit too wild, even for the Beatles, who thought they had seen it all. Before the show, one of their assistants had been bitten by a fan who also jumped on the hood of her car. Hearing about the incident made John nervous. Paul had much the same reaction when he saw "the dreadful crush of fans up against the stage." A stampede of teenagers had broken through the barricades and surged forward, wave after wave, attempting to vault onto the stage. "Calm down!" Paul screamed at them. "Things are getting dangerous." He even stopped the show midway through so that police could rescue a woman who was being trampled.

Eventually, the Beatles had seen enough and bolted, leaving Ringo to speak for the rest of the band. "We survived," he told an interviewer. "That's the important thing, wouldn't you say?"

· · · · ·

Having survived, the Beatles took a well-deserved vacation, giving them time to settle into new homes, see friends, and *sleep.* Beatlemania raged on without them. Their records were all over the radio, while Paul's single of "Yesterday" captured the top spot on the Hot 100 for four weeks running. The only action during the rare break came on September 13, 1965, when Ringo's wife, Maureen, gave birth to a boy, whom they named Zak. "I won't let Zak be a drummer!" Ringo declared to reporters outside the hospital delivery room, but twenty years later, Zak would handle that very job for the Who. Otherwise, Paul tore around London, gorging himself on culture. ("I *must* know what people are doing," he said, in between visiting art galleries, taking piano lessons, and listening to experimental music.) And George took time out in January 1966 to marry his girlfriend, Pattie, which left Paul as the only bachelor in the band.

Ringo and Maureen in 1965, greeting the press after their wedding. © MIRRORPIX

In the meantime, the Beatles' record company wanted a new album in time for the holiday season. That meant John and Paul had to come up with a dozen new songs in a little more than two weeks, which seemed like an impossible feat, even for such naturals.

One thing was certain: this record wasn't going to sound like anything they'd ever done before. There was too much going on in the rock music scene. Paul spoke for the others when he complained of "being bored by doing the same thing." The Beatles had moved on creatively. "You can't be singing fifteen-year-old songs at twenty because you don't think fifteen-year-old thoughts at twenty," Paul explained. "We were suddenly hearing sounds that we weren't able to hear before," George observed.

Help!

John plowed tremendous emotional upheaval into his songs. He said "Help!" grew out of one of the "deep depressions" he went through, during which he fought the desire "to jump out the window." He wasn't speaking literally; the people closest to John never recall any suicidal tendencies. But his dissatisfaction with the direction the Beatles were taking, coupled with his frustrating marriage, left him feeling despondent and "hopeless" during the song's writing.

Ringo Starr behind the camera during the filming of *Help!* on Salisbury Plain. © MIRRORPIX

"I was fat and depressed and I *was* crying out for help," John insisted later on. "He was feeling a bit constricted by the Beatle thing," Paul observed. But at the time he began writing "Help!" it was fashioned as a title song for the band's new movie of that name. Paul was summoned to John's house especially "to complete it," he recalled, which they did without delay, nailing it in one two-hour session in the upstairs music room.

As everyone well knew, the summer of 1965 had produced a rich vein of exceptional hit singles, notable for their originality and authenticity. Bob Dylan had started the ball rolling, not only with "Like a Rolling Stone" but also the Byrds' version of "Mr. Tambourine Man," which he had written. The Animals, a London band, offered the bluesy "We Gotta Get Out of This Place," followed by the Who's "My Generation" and the Yardbirds' "For Your Love." And nothing stood up to the Rolling Stones' two smash hits, "The Last Time" and "Satisfaction."

Such great competition turned out to be all the incentive John and Paul needed. Throughout the first few weeks of October, new songs were ripped off their guitars one right after the other, each as different and original as the last. There was nothing predictable about songs like "Norwegian Wood," "Drive My Car," "Nowhere Man," or "In My Life." Paul had also been noodling around with "Michelle." It was clear they had another hit on their hands.

The album, named *Rubber Soul,* "broke everything open," according to rocker Steve Winwood. "It crossed music into a whole new dimension and was responsible for kicking off the sixties rock era as we know it." Almost every music fan echoed his opinion that the Beatles had "raised the bar" in a way that made musicians reconsider how they wrote and recorded songs. Even *Newsweek,* which two years earlier had ridiculed the Beatles' haircuts and unlikely talent, now called them the "Bards of Pop" and their songs "as brilliantly original as any written today."

In just three short years, the Beatles had gone from long-haired rebels to international idols, cutting across age groups and cultures. Fans and critics wondered where they could go from here. Would they rock harder, louder, or perhaps looser? It was anyone's guess.

No one imagined the actual outcome. Because in time, the Beatles got weird—very weird.

Chapter 9

THE END **OF BEATLEMANIA**

The Beatles had always gone all out to make great-sounding songs; now it was time, they decided, to make great-sounding albums. The trouble was, Abbey Road was still in the dark ages as far as technical practices were concerned. The four-track machines used to record every artist from the London Philharmonic orchestra to Herman's Hermits were regarded as dinosaurs elsewhere in the world. And it frustrated the Beatles no end.

To complicate matters, the band's two primary songwriters, John and Paul, were working on material that required more advanced techniques in everything from musicianship to recording. John, in particular, had roughed out the blueprint for a song he mysteriously called "Mark 1" that screamed out for unusual sound effects. Some of the lyrics were taken from ideas in *The Tibetan Book of the Dead.* "Whenever in doubt," he had read, "turn off your mind, relax, and float downstream." The whole concept was irresistible to John for many reasons. Rushing home, he took some LSD. Almost immediately, the words came: long, strange strings of words started threading around gauzy ideas.

He played it for Paul, who hadn't yet experimented with LSD, during a meeting at Brian Epstein's flat. Incredibly, it "was all on the chord of C," according to Paul. Somehow, John had stripped the music to its most basic structure. Paul was intrigued but wondered how George Martin would deal with it, especially considering the Beatles' reputation for churning out melodic four-chord hits. To his credit, Martin "didn't flinch at all when John played it to him," Paul recalled. "He just said, 'Hmm, I see, yes. Hmm, hmm." Martin thought it was "rather interesting," according to Paul.

The Beatles on the set of *Top of the Pops*, June 16, 1966. © MIRRORPIX

Interesting but unfinished. The lyric was only two verses and the melody just one chord. "We worked very hard to stretch it into two verses," Paul explained. "We racked our brains but couldn't come up with any more words because we felt it already said everything we wanted to say in the two verses." Still, they had to find a way to make it longer while still preserving its originality.

Paul came up with the solution: tape loops. He'd discovered a process whereby if he removed a piece from the tape recorder and replaced it with a loop of recording tape, he could play a short phrase or sound that would go round and round, overdubbing itself, which made a funny sound. Moreover, the loops could be played at various speeds, as well as backward and forward. He demonstrated this for the others in the studio, encouraging George and Ringo to make loops as well.

John loved the loop concept for "Mark 1" and discussed several ideas for the vocal, each one crazier than the next. "He wanted his voice to sound like the Dalai Lama chanting from the hilltop," George Martin recalled. Most producers would have dismissed such an idea out of hand, but Martin, a wise and patient man, gave the Beatles enormous leeway. Their ideas might have sounded weird *initially,* but he recognized that because of their lack of formal musical training, they often just needed someone to translate what they meant, to express it in terms that made sense to sound technicians. Which is where he came in: he was their unofficial translator.

Martin set to work to create some kind of a Tibetan effect in the studio. But John's next suggestion—that "we suspend him from a rope in the middle of the studio ceiling, put a mike in the middle of the floor, give him a push, and he'd sing as he went around and around"—was met with a barely tolerant smile.

Eventually, their engineer came up with an inventive idea they loved. He put John's voice through an organ speaker and re-recorded it as it came back out. This gave John's voice a vibrato effect, which was a revolutionary sound. Such innovation was considered taboo at Abbey Road, where engineers were discouraged from playing around with the equipment. "I remember the surprise on our faces when the voice came out of the speaker," the engineer recalled. The Beatles were beside themselves with glee. They realized that the possibilities were limitless. Recording was no longer just a way of putting out songs but a new way of creating them.

Once the Beatles got their hands on the controls, they found it impossible to leave them alone. "The group encouraged us to break the rules," the engineer said. They felt that "every instrument should sound unlike itself." As well as each of the Beatles. John flirted with the idea of having "thousands of monks chanting" in the background of "Mark 1." That was highly unlikely, but a way to simulate it was to double-track John's voice—that is, to re-record John singing and to superimpose the recording over the original.

John was especially "knocked out" by the sound. He made up a goofy name for the effect, calling it "a double-bifurcated sploshing flange." *A sploshing flange!* And from that point on, the technique known throughout the recording industry as "flanging" was practiced.

After listening to the spooky-sounding "Mark 1," which they eventually retitled

"Tomorrow Never Knows," it was inevitable that the Beatles would want to tinker in some way with every new song. For instance, on "Rain," John threaded a tape of the vocal onto the recorder and played it *backward.* The sound was unlike anything he'd ever heard before, a piercing *scronnnch whuppp-whuppp-whuppp* interspersed with wailing feedback. Everyone in the studio reveled in the process, running instrument and vocal tapes in every direction. They used it on "Taxman" and throughout George's guitar solo on "I'm Only Sleeping." At some point, however, it got out of hand. "And that was awful," George Martin recalled, "because everything we did after that was backwards. Every guitar solo was backwards, and they tried to think backwards in writing."

Backward or forward, the work was producing amazing results. There was a sense of real adventure—and real accomplishment—in the studio. It seemed as though ideas were ricocheting off the walls. "We were really starting to find ourselves in the studio," Ringo observed. Some of the magic, of course, was the result of drugs, with which they were all experimenting to various degrees, but somehow the Beatles' focus remained razor sharp. "We were really hard workers...we worked like dogs to get it right."

Recording now occupied almost all of their time, which made it difficult for the band to get up for playing gigs. The excuse they gave was: "It was too much trouble to fight our way through all the screaming hordes of people to [lip-synch] to the latest single." But the truth was, it was becoming harder to reproduce onstage the kind of effects-heavy music they were creating in the studio. Foot pedals for guitars were still a few years off, and there were no remote sound-mixing boards or monitors then. Their new songs, like "Eleanor Rigby" and "Tomorrow Never Knows," contained sounds that could be made only in the studio. There was no way they could play them live. And yet, they had to find a way to publicize their new single, "Paperback Writer" and "Rain."

No one recalls who came up with the solution, but sometime in early May 1966, the Beatles decided to make amusing promotional films of both songs—lip-synched versions set to comical scenes not unlike those in *A Hard Day's Night.* The films would be sent out to TV stations in place of live performances. "I don't think we even thought of calling them

158

'videos,'" Ringo speculated, but videos indeed they were—the first of their kind, and eighteen years ahead of their explosion into the forefront of pop culture.

• • • • •

By the beginning of June 1966, the Beatles were putting the finishing touches on their new album, *Revolver,* which was perceived by them as representing "a new British sound," if not a brilliant leap forward. "Taxman," with its looping bass lines and savage guitar solo, was an amazing contribution from George Harrison, who was becoming quite a talented songwriter. And earlier that month, "Eleanor Rigby" had been given the full symphonic treatment, featuring a double string quartet: four violins, two violas, and two cellos.

The Beatles let their hair down for one of the album's final tracks. On "Yellow Submarine" they gave a comic edge to a children's song Paul had written by layering it with wisecracks and sound effects from childhood. The studio's vast wooden floor was littered with noisemaking devices, including chains, ship's bells, handbells, tap-dancing mats, whistles, wind machines, thunderstorm machines—every oddity they could lay their hands on. A cash register was dragged out, along with several buckets, a set of bar glasses, even an old metal bathtub that was promptly filled with water.

The Beatles and George Martin at Abbey Road studio.
© MICHAEL OCHS ARCHIVES/REDFERNS

YEAH! **YEAH! YEAH!**

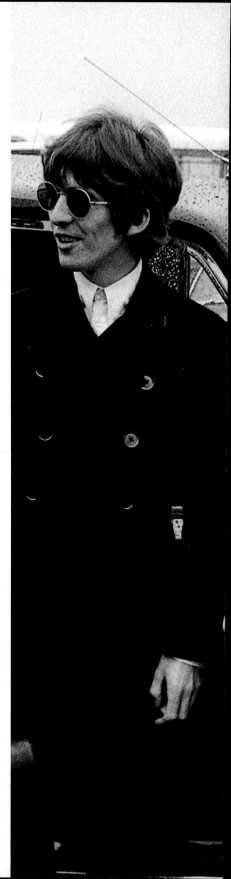

"They had a whole crowd of people to do the effects," recalled their engineer. Friends, wives, and girlfriends were recruited to rattle and clink various hardware. The Beatles' chauffeur swirled chains through the bath, junior engineers made whooshing noises. Everyone laughed and hooted as the tape captured the hijinks. At some point, after hours of overdubs, one of the band's equipment men strapped on a bass drum and, bashing away, led a conga line around the cluttered studio while everyone chanted the memorable chorus: *"We all live in a yellow submarine..."* It was party time at Abbey Road.

• • • • •

But soon enough it was back to work for another world tour.

Flying was part of the Beatles' job description, and on June 27 they were back in the air, en route to Japan. A fierce storm raging in the China Sea forced them to stop in Alaska until the danger passed. Nearly twenty hours later, the plane landed in the middle of the night at Tokyo's Haneda Airport, where the storm may have passed, but not the danger. The Beatles were greeted by a plainclothes police commissioner who warned them about threats against the band by a Japanese cult. If the Beatles played in a certain arena where no Westerner had ever set foot, he told them, it was said they would not leave Tokyo alive.

None of the Beatles took the threat seriously—but the Japanese authorities did. As a result, the boys had an armed motorcycle escort wherever they went in Tokyo. Security was even tighter at the Tokyo Hilton, which was turned into an armed camp. All the

The Beatles arrive at Heathrow Airport to fly out on another tour, 1966. © MIRRORPIX

bedrooms around them were allocated for the police. "We were locked up in the hotel for a long time," recalled Paul. The Beatles were irritable and growing increasingly restless. "It was their first time in the Far East," said a business associate, "and they'd been looking forward to getting out. They resented being cooped up like zoo animals."

The trip to the concert hall was even more difficult. "We had to go under about twenty bridges, which is where all the police stood with guns," remembered a colleague. Fans were kept in penlike structures at specific points along the route and under armed guard. Throughout the trip, the Beatles were mostly silent, gazing at the scenery, trying to get a feeling for where they were. Everything looked so different and strange. It was unlike anything they'd experienced before.

Things really began to unravel in the Philippines. First of all, when the Beatles disembarked from the plane they were put on a boat until their belongings cleared Customs and their hotel room was ready. "We were all sweating and frightened," recalled George. Security was tight; a quarter of Manila's police force had been detailed for Beatles duty.

Meanwhile, a note attached to their itinerary indicated that they were to call on the First Lady, Imelda Marcos, at the palace before their first concert. The Beatles' policy was *never* to go to government functions, so Brian Epstein declined the invitation. The next morning, a general and a commander from the Philippine army, both in crisply starched uniforms, showed up at the hotel to make final arrangements for the Beatles to attend the palace function. "We'll do nothing of the sort," Brian informed them. "We're not going to go."

The trouble started later that day. The Beatles played a rousing show to an enthusiastic audience of 35,000 fans under a blistering sun. Back at the hotel before the evening show, they turned on the TV to watch coverage of their concert. On one channel, there was footage of the palace, showing how invited guests had waited but been stood up by the Beatles. An announcer implied that the Beatles had insulted President and Mrs. Marcos.

Things got ugly after the Beatles' evening performance. For one thing, their police escort disappeared. Then, when their car pulled up to the hotel gates, it was clear they had been locked out. As if on cue, several dozen troublemakers converged on the car, banging on the windows and rocking the vehicle. Finally, their car rammed the gates. As they raced to the hotel entrance, doors flew open, and everyone then ran into the hotel, two steps ahead of the angry throng.

At the hotel, the staff now refused to provide them with room service, and their phones had been shut off. Then "things started to get really weird," as Ringo recalled it. When they tried to leave the hotel, the elevators had been shut off. The halls were dark but lined with hotel staff shouting threats at the Beatles in Spanish and English. "It was very, very frightening," one of their entourage recalled. When they got

George receiving instruction in playing the sitar as the other members of the Beatles look on, July 5, 1966. © BETTMANN/CORBIS

downstairs, the lobby was deserted, with no security in sight. Even their cars were gone.

"Nobody would give us a ride," George recalled. Someone managed to get them a car, but the drive to the airport was sabotaged by soldiers who kept motioning their car onto ramps that led in circles. Inside the terminal, the airline desks were empty and the escalators were shut off. On the tarmac, a crowd of two hundred men, many in military uniform, had gathered, waving pistols or clutching clubs. "Nobody was helping us do anything," George remembered, "but people were trying to grab us, and other people were trying to hit us." Police shoved them from one side of the room to the other, like a game of Ping-Pong using the Beatles. According to Ringo, "They started spitting at us, spitting *on* us."

After about fifteen minutes, everyone was allowed to run across the tarmac to the plane. The terrified Beatles climbed the stairs into the cabin. It was hot, over ninety degrees, but they were relieved. Once the plane was in the air, the Beatles were unusually quiet. Whatever the reasons for the situation, they decided, it mustn't ever happen again.

From the moment they landed in India, so George could buy a sitar, an Indian string instrument, the Beatles discussed the possibility of not touring again. Ever. "Who needs this?" was an oft-heard lament. They were tired of simply going through the motions, tired of acting like the four wax dummies sent out to satisfy the crowds. "I prefer to be out of the public eye anyway," George said. After Shea Stadium, John had never hidden his dislike for stadiums filled with screaming kids. They agreed that it was unlikely the Beatles would tour again.

Brian heard these rumblings and fell into a dark mood. To make matters worse, the flight home was awful; several of the Beatles got food poisoning. When they landed, everyone went their separate ways for a rest. But on the fourth day, just as Brian had settled in comfortably at a beachside getaway, he got a call from one of his assistants in London. You'd better get back immediately, she told him. They had real trouble on their hands.

Sparked by John's comment that the Beatles were more popular than Jesus, young fans in Waycross, Georgia, prepare to burn albums at a bonfire in protest, August 1966. © BETTMANN/CORBIS

· · · · ·

"Christianity will go. It will vanish and shrink...." The words sounded vaguely familiar to Brian as he listened to a telegram. "We're more popular than Jesus now."

It was part of a newspaper interview that John had given a few months back. They were just a few old offhand remarks, not really serious, but a cheesy American magazine had reprinted them in a sensational way, taking them out of context, with sleazy-sounding headlines. The reaction was predictable. Some disc jockeys in the South banned the playing of all Beatles records and sponsored a community bonfire so people could burn their albums. Things grew even more ridiculous. One station in Texas "damned their songs eternally." A minister in Cleveland threatened to revoke the membership of anyone in the congregation who played Beatles records. Boycotts were announced in communities in Kentucky, Georgia, Mississippi, South Carolina, and upstate New York. And word had it that nutcases were threatening to assassinate John Lennon if the Beatles came to Memphis, one of the scheduled stops of the upcoming American tour.

The Beatles, according to Paul, "didn't really take it too seriously at all." Brian publicly called the controversy "a storm in a teacup." Even John said, "I'd forgotten all about it." Nevertheless, Brian persuaded John to apologize for his remarks. There was too much at stake, he argued, with another American tour set to begin in just a few weeks. "And in the end," Ringo said, "John realized that he'd have to go out and do it."

Even after John's public apology, however, the tour was tension packed. The Beatles hadn't wanted to do the tour in the first place, but Brian had talked them into it. "By the time we got to Memphis," a colleague remembered, "there was a strong rumor that something truly violent could happen." Brian was very nervous. "He was convinced some nut was going to take a shot at John," his lawyer recalled. There had been some discussions about canceling the Memphis concert, but the Beatles insisted on appearing. "If we cancel one, you might as well as cancel all of them," Paul insisted.

John wore a troubled look as their plane made its descent into Memphis. "You are

"Taxman"

Like many topical songs, "Taxman" sprang from anger and disillusionment. After the success of *Help!*, George endured a despairing meeting with the Beatles' accountants. "I had discovered I was paying a huge amount of money to the taxman," complained George. "Well, I don't want to *pay* tax. It's not *fair.*"

George's response would open the *Revolver* album. Everything is taxable, according to the accountant in the song: the street, your seat, the heat, your feet. No matter what you do or how much you have—*pay up and shut up.* And it doesn't stop there. After you are dead, he advises listeners, be sure to "declare the pennies on your eyes."

"Taxman" was as sly and critical as anything that was being written. And of course John threw in a few one-liners to help the song along, accompanied by Paul's looping bass lines and the song's signature guitar solo.

As far as first-rate songwriting went, with "Taxman," George had arrived.

a very controversial person," Paul said to him, without his usual cheery note. Only George managed to shed some humor on the situation as they taxied to a stop. "Send John out first," he quipped. "He's the one they want."

Their first show went off like any other. There was the typical pandemonium, plenty of crying and screaming; girls littered the stage with stuffed animals and other gifts. Understandably, the Beatles' mood improved. "Everyone started to relax," recalled an observer. The second show was also packed with more than twelve thousand delirious kids. It was a great rave-up, until midway through the third song, "If I Needed Someone," when a shot rang out. Brian, who was standing at the side of the stage, crouched down. Paul and George jerked sideways toward John, who was straddling the mike. Later, Paul explained to a reporter how "when he heard [the blast] his heart stopped, but he realized he was still standing and didn't feel anything. He looked at John and saw that he was still standing, so they all kept right on playing."

Kids. Two teenagers had lobbed a cherry bomb from the upper balcony.

The Beatles fought back. Their playing was

166

unusually sharp, full of snap and bite, and for the moment they gave it all they had. But they were put off by the whole crazy atmosphere. George especially was fed up with the chaotic life of the Beatles. In discussions with friends, he talked of feeling "wasted" and virtually "imprisoned" by Beatlemania. The touring had beat him up. "It had been four years of legging around in screaming mania," he grumbled. He was bored and dispirited.

"Nobody was listening at the shows," complained Ringo, who said he "was fed up with playing" in such a haphazard manner. It was impossible for him to hear what the others were doing onstage, forcing him to play along to their movements rather than the music. Ringo had always been a sport; he'd always done whatever was asked of him, whatever was best for the band. He'd played the role that was required of him, but his heart wasn't in it anymore.

And to John, the whole scene was a dreadful experience. "I didn't want to tour again," he said. He had had it with playing crazy gigs. Besides, he felt the music was stale. "I couldn't take it anymore," he said.

Ringo Starr and Paul McCartney look out an aircraft window. © Mirrorpix

A series of accidents in Cincinnati and St. Louis underscored the Beatles' distaste for the road. Cincinnati was a disaster. It rained before showtime as the Beatles arrived at Crosley Field, but with a ballpark full of soggy fans determined to see their idols, the boys seemed inclined to appear despite the weather. "They'd brought in the electricity," George recalled, "but the stage was soaking, and we would have been electrocuted." The crowd kept screaming, *"We want the Beatles!"* Paul grew so upset at the prospect of going on stage that he got sick in the dressing room. Eventually, Brian called off the show—"the only one we ever missed," George pointed out—but they played a makeup the next day before flying out.

The weather followed them to St. Louis. "There were sparks flying all over the place," recalled a stagehand. "Every time Paul bumped into the mike, which was almost every beat, there were sparks." After the show, during a narrow escape inside the container of a chrome-paneled truck, all the damage finally caught up with the Beatles. "We were sliding around trying to hold on to something," Paul recalled, "and at that moment everyone" decided they'd had enough of touring. There was no point in pretending anymore. Even Paul admitted he'd had enough; the touring, to him, "had become spiritually rather empty." The Beatles would make more than enough money from continued record sales as well as other projects that came along. It was time to call it quits—and easier to walk away now, while they were still on top.

"We didn't make a formal announcement that we were going to stop touring," Ringo recalled. Nevertheless, the matter was settled among them. The concert in San Francisco would be their last. There would be no more Beatles shows, no more participation in the lunacy of Beatlemania. From now on, they would exist solely in the studio as a band that made records.

Candlestick Park was a notoriously windswept arena, with its outfield facing onto San Francisco Bay, but that Monday night, August 29, gusts whipped through the stands with a vengeance. Banners strung around the stadium flapped ferociously against the squall, and drafts picked up great clouds of dust and blew them volcanically across the infield.

The stands were only half filled, with 25,000 Beatles fans huddled against the cold.

The performance itself was nothing extraordinary. The Beatles sang eleven songs—the same eleven totally familiar studio-recorded versions they'd been singing for four years, with one or two exceptions—using the same patter, the same tired jokes. "The boys were very tired indeed and couldn't wait to get that last show over," recalled their press manager. John had nothing left in his tank. He didn't hesitate for a moment when it came to leading the charge off the field and disappearing with the others into a waiting armored truck. A great feeling of release washed over him as the van kicked up dust, speeding toward the right-field bullpen, toward the end of Beatlemania.

George also sighed and settled into the momentous finale. "I was thinking, 'This is going to be such a relief—not to have to go through this madness anymore,'" he recalled. There was an air of satisfaction as their plane took off for Los Angeles. Sinking into the seat next to their press manager, George closed his eyes, smiled, and said, "Right—that's it. I'm not a Beatle anymore."

Chapter 10

Not touring anymore brought the Beatles no instant peace. Instead of giving them the kind of quiet they had hoped for, the whole world took up their case, talking around the clock about the Beatles and wondering about their future. Were they finished? And at such young ages, barely in their midtwenties? "Is Beatlemania Dead?" *Time* magazine wondered at the end of 1966. Even the band's closest friends didn't have the answer. Certainly *Revolver* had defied all predictions and won vast popular acclaim. It was packed with great songs, including "Eleanor Rigby," "Good Day Sunshine," and "Got to Get You into My Life," and sold millions of copies while giving fans and musicians alike something extraordinary.

In July, John was offered a minor role in a new movie comedy called *How I Won the War*. He not only agreed but promised to cut his famous hair to a length befitting a proper English soldier. But working as a supporting actor proved excruciatingly boring. In Germany and southern Spain, where most of the action was filmed, John spent most of his time just "hanging around," waiting for his scenes to be called. To kill time, John relied on his guitar. Music would provide for him. It always had. "He used to sit cross-legged on the beach or on the bed, working out a melody," recalled Michael Crawford, who costarred in the film and shared a house with John. It was there, Crawford said, "I heard him playing the same bar over and over again." *"Living is easy with eyes closed, misunderstanding all you see..."* The tune had a dreamy feel to it. Crawford was struck by its beauty. "Really, it's good," he told John. "I wouldn't mess with it."

With "Strawberry Fields Forever," which that bar of music later became, John took his songwriting to the next level. The song was about a field in Woolton, the scene of his favorite childhood adventures, where he spent blissful mornings playing in Calderstones Park with his friends. Strawberry Field (John added the *s*) wasn't a patch of land but the name of an old Victorian house, converted for Salvation Army orphans, near the entrance to the park. "There was something about the place that always fascinated John," Aunt Mimi recalled. "He could see it from his window, and he loved going to the garden party they had each year." All those childhood memories came flooding back as John amused himself in Spain, working on a song that was among the most famous he ever wrote.

Paul was also abroad, in France, where he took the sightseer's route from Paris through the Loire Valley. His intention was to "travel incognito, disguised so that he would not be recognized," or at least appear as inconspicuous as any young man traveling across France in a $150,000 Aston Martin DB5 sports car. Slicking his hair back with Vaseline and gluing a fake beard to his chin, Paul managed to walk freely around the quaint villages, browsing in

Paul returning from a holiday in France. Aboard his return flight he hit upon the concept for their new album: salt and pepper—Sergeant Pepper. © Mirrorpix

little shops and dining outside at neighborhood cafés—something the Beatles never could have done.

But on the airplane home after a two-week safari in Kenya, Paul McCartney changed back into SuperBeatle. He began formulating an idea for a new Beatles album. He figured that if *he* could disguise himself and travel about unnoticed, then why not all the Beatles? They hated being the Fab Four, a nickname that had become synonymous with Beatlemania. "I thought, 'Let's not be ourselves,'" Paul said. Let's do something that could "put some distance between the Beatles and the public," perhaps take on the personality of another, made-up band.

Paul and Mal Evans, one of the Beatles' roadies, kicked around the idea during the inflight meal. At first, they played with names for a band, mimicking the groups that were just coming into vogue like the Bonzo Dog Doo-Dah Band, Big Brother and the Holding Company, Lothar and the Hand People. Evans, distracted, picked up the little paper packets marked *S* and *P,* asking Paul what the initials stood for. "Salt and pepper," he responded. "Sergeant Pepper."

By the time the plane touched down in London, the entire concept was in place.

• • • • •

It was difficult at first for the other Beatles to understand Paul's idea: an album *made* by the Beatles but *not* the Beatles. Would it be Beatles music? they wondered. "We would be Sgt. Pepper's band, and for the whole album we'd pretend to be someone else," Paul explained.

George wasn't sure. He thought it sounded too much like a gimmick. Part of the problem was that George's tastes were changing. He had become fascinated with Eastern culture, spirituality, and Indian music. "The first time I heard Indian music," George recalled, "I felt as though I *knew* it. It was like every music I had ever heard, but twenty times better than everything all put together. It was just so strong, so overwhelmingly positive, it buzzed me

173

"Lucy in the Sky with Diamonds"

One of the Beatles' best songs was inspired by a "blurry and watery" painting John's son Julian brought home from nursery school. "The top was all dark blue sky with some very rough-looking stars, [and] green grass along the bottom," Julian recalled years later. Near the corner, he'd drawn a stick-figure girl—presumably his classmate Lucy O'Donnell, identified by her long blond hair. "I showed it to Dad, and he said, 'What's that, then?'" Julian blurted out the first thing that came into his mind: "That's Lucy in the sky, you know, with diamonds."

John with son Julian, age five. © Bettmann/CORBIS

right out of my brain." It changed him in other ways, too. Meditation and yoga became a part of his daily routine. He transformed his home, filling it with brightly colored Indian artifacts and repositioning the furniture for maximum peacefulness. Long, flowing robes replaced his customary T-shirts and jeans. So an idea like Paul's—that they become another band called Sgt. Pepper's—sounded silly to George, who said, "I wasn't really that *into* it."

John, too, was a bit skeptical, but he agreed to go along with it. Only Ringo was completely behind the idea, thinking, "Anything could happen, and that was an exciting process."

Whatever their reasoning, one thing was certain: pop music was changing in a radical new manner, and the Beatles were determined to lead the way. Rock 'n roll, which was once only about cars, girls, and school, had become music for "serious" fans, and the level of artistry that fans expected from the records they bought got ever higher. Groups like the Doors and the psychedelic boogie bands put listeners on notice that rock music was growing up. Within the next few years, they would be joined by virtually all the 1960s rock greats: Pink Floyd, Janis Joplin, Traffic, Jethro Tull, Sly and the Family Stone, the Jefferson Airplane, Elton John, Creedence Clearwater Revival, the Allman Brothers, Joni Mitchell, and Led Zeppelin, as well as the great soul groups—all of them riding the coattails of the Mersey sound created by the Beatles.

Throughout the first four months of 1967, the Beatles remained in Abbey Road, working steadily, fussily, on the new album. Never had they enjoyed such a luxury of time to record. In the past, there had always been a last-minute crunch to write enough songs and get them recorded before the next tour began. But now, at last, they had time, precious time. No deadlines, no tours, no movies, no *nothing*.

George Martin always considered the studio to be the Beatles' "playground," but a

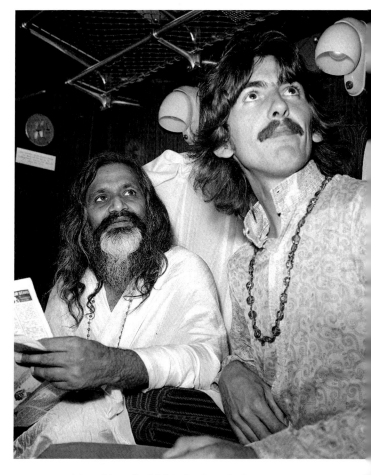

George Harrison with Maharishi Mahesh Yogi, 1967. © MIRRORPIX

laboratory was more like it. No song was safe. Ideas that once might have been polished off in a day or two were turned inside out and upside down to see what would happen. At home following a long night's work, John, Paul, or George might listen to a tape of the day's session, pick up a guitar, and bang out an idea that sent everyone back to the drawing board. Immediately, this experimentation began to pay off.

By the middle of January, they began work on the epic "A Day in the Life." This was

no ordinary song. Even in the early run-through, it showed unmistakable brilliance. The gorgeous melody, as stark as it is soulful, stands as one of the Beatles' finest accomplishments. But there were twenty-four bars of music in the middle that had been left blank. Something would materialize, they figured—it always did. Finally, it dawned on Paul: a big orchestra buildup. "It was a crazy song, anyway," he said. Explaining it to John, he said, "We'll tell the orchestra to start on whatever the lowest note on their instrument is, and to arrive at the highest note on their instrument. But to do it in their own time." The effect, he said, "would be something really startling."

When Paul told George Martin to hire a symphony orchestra, the producer told him to forget it. He liked Paul's idea, "but ninety musicians"—the standard symphony—"would be too expensive." After thinking it over, they settled on *half* an orchestra—forty-one musicians from the prestigious London Philharmonic—to play twenty-four bars of music. It was a ridiculous expense, but it was for the Beatles, after all.

On February 10, the orchestra, all in tuxedos, assembled in Abbey Road Studio One, a hall as big as an airplane hangar. The Beatles distributed gag accessories to the horrified musicians: the violinists got red clown noses, the conductor was fitted with a fake gorilla's paw, balloons were attached to the bows of the stringed instruments, the brass and woodwind sections wore funny hats and plastic glasses with fake noses. John giddily handed out fake cigars. "People were running around with sparklers and blowing bubbles through little clay pipes," George Martin recalled. To many of the musicians, it was an undignified way to behave, and

The Beatles promote their new album, *Sergeant Pepper*, 1967. © Mirrorpix they were offended, but they all soon got into the spirit.

Once the musicians got their instructions, they played the crazy piece of music, with each instrument swirling higher and higher up the scale, creating a monster symphonic effect. But the high note that was reached at the end of the sequence just dangled there. It needed an end. After much discussion, they settled on playing "a gigantic piano chord" that would echo for just over a minute. The staff rolled three grand pianos into the studio, and on the count of four, ten hands clamped down on a single chord as hard as humanly possible, letting it reverberate through the hall. It was a magnificent, stirring effect, as final as it was dramatic, that served to punctuate one of the Beatles' outstanding studio performances.

In a little over three weeks, the Beatles laid down the basic tracks for "Fixing a Hole," "Being for the Benefit of Mr. Kite!" "Good Morning, Good Morning," "Lovely Rita," "Getting Better," and "She's Leaving Home." The recording staff at Abbey Road had never experienced anything like it. The engineers were kept on their toes, trying to create the

The *Sgt. Pepper's Lonely Hearts Club Band* Cover

Artist Peter Blake told the Beatles they could have anyone they want appear in a group shot on the cover of *Sgt. Pepper's Lonely Hearts Club Band*.

Anyone? The idea tantalized the Beatles, who loved the prankish quality of it. "Anyone" meant friends or heroes or family or, well, any face that tickled their fancy. Let the fans go crazy trying to figure out who was in the crowd and why. What a hoot it would be, they decided.

The Beatles made lists of the people they'd like to include. George's list was the strangest: it featured eight Indian holy men, including the Maharishi Mahesh Yogi. Paul went mostly for artsy choices, like the writers William Burroughs, Aldous Huxley, and Alfred Jarry, dancer Fred Astaire, comedian Groucho Marx, the artist Magritte, and a locally famous footballer named Dixie Dean. John, true to character, wanted to stir up trouble and chose Hitler, then Gandhi (neither of whom made it onto the final cover), philosopher Friedrich Nietzsche, and writers Oscar Wilde, H. G. Wells, Edgar Allan Poe, and Lewis Carroll. And, for good measure, Jesus, who seemed to John like a "naughty" choice. When Blake collected the names, only Ringo hesitated. "Whatever the others have is fine by me," he replied. "I won't put anyone in."

extraordinary effects that caromed around in the Beatles' heads. How about speeding up the tape to play havoc with the vocals? they wondered. (They accomplished just that on "When I'm Sixty-four.") Or slowing it down? (On "Lucy in the Sky with Diamonds" the tape was delayed.) Nothing was sacred.

One of the most enterprising tracks was "Being for the Benefit of Mr. Kite!" John was explicit about the atmosphere: he wanted a "fairground sound," something that jogged his memory of wandering through village fairs where one could "smell the sawdust" and hear the crowd amid the background racket of the arcade. George Martin put out a call for a steam organ. The cost of renting and programming one was prohibitive, he discovered, even for his golden boys. Instead, they created their own backing track—"a pumping kind of sound," Martin called it—with other kinds of organs and a harmonica overdub. Over a six-hour marathon, Paul played various keyboards, John contributed the oompahpahs on an organ, and Martin pumped the harmonium nonstop until he literally gave out, collapsing on the floor from exhaustion. Almost magically, a fairground sound materialized. "John was thrilled to bits with it," Martin recalled.

By the third week in April, the Beatles had

The Beatles at Brian Epstein's home to launch the *Sgt. Pepper* album, May 1967. © Mirrorpix

reached the end of their *Sgt. Pepper's Lonely Hearts Club Band* odyssey. They had logged slightly more than five months in the studio, unheard of, considering that when they began making records everything had to be done in one day. Now the Beatles batted around ideas for an album cover that would complement the music. The situation, they agreed, called for something fresh, daring, and grand: unusual art, psychedelic design, an entertaining sleeve, and extra goodies. One of the project coordinators suggested printing the lyrics to the songs inside the album cover, over pictures of the Beatles. *Lyrics!* It had never been done. As routine as this practice seems now, the idea was revolutionary. "We wanted the sleeve to be really interesting," Paul insisted. "Everyone agreed."

Paul and Linda Eastman locked eyes early at the press listening for *Sgt. Pepper's Lonely Hearts Club Band*, at Brian Epstein's flat in May 1967. © Hulton-Deutsch Collection/Corbis

One thing was certain: there wouldn't be a standard photograph of the four Beatles on the cover. *Sgt. Pepper* demanded a bold new look. Paul had made sketches of the Beatles dressed in Salvation Army–type band uniforms, standing in front of framed photographs of their heroes. The other Beatles approved of his concept. A professional designer instructed each of the Beatles to make a list of people whose photographs they'd like to feature on the cover. The names they proposed included artists, actors, writers, rock 'n rollers, philosophers, and an athlete. At the last minute, John, to his credit, insisted they include Stuart Sutcliffe. Before they were finished, the Beatles created a souvenir cutout kit, with a Sgt. Pepper's bass drum, mustaches, and badges that could

180

be slipped into the album. The whole thing came together in less than two weeks' time.

For all their confidence, the Beatles worried about public and critical reaction as the release of *Sgt. Pepper's Lonely Hearts Club Band* drew near. "I was downright scared," George Martin admitted, "but not half as worried as the Beatles."

May 19, 1967, was launch day. It was time to put some of their worries to the test. To celebrate the occasion, a small press party was held at Brian Epstein's town house. The invitation list was handpicked: a dozen top-tier journalists, a dozen photographers, half as many influential deejays, and of course the Beatles. Champagne flowed freely as everyone awaited the Beatles' grand entrance. They were still upstairs in a photo session, having fun with the photographers, who were all familiar faces. Except one, that is.

Linda Eastman was an American photographer. She was twenty-five, a little older than Paul, with a portfolio jammed with rock stars in various candid poses. Not many women had broken into this profession, but Linda had several things going for her. Tall and willowy, with a natural milk-and-honey complexion, she was the kind of strikingly pretty girl who could nonetheless put guys at ease with a quick grin and an easy, outgoing manner.

Paul had met Linda four days before the party, at an exclusive London disco. He was instantly smitten with her and had spent the entire night talking to her about art. Now, at the album launch, he couldn't help but admire her beauty and spunk. Linda had come dressed to kill, in an expensive double-breasted striped barbershop jacket over a sheer black sweater, with a miniskirt that flattered her gorgeous legs. A photograph taken of Paul and Linda during this encounter reveals their powerful attraction. Anyone standing nearby couldn't help but notice that something was happening between them. He vowed to see her later and asked for her number. Of course, there was an obstacle: he was still dating Jane Asher. But they were drifting apart, due to Jane's busy career and Paul's wandering eye. And for the moment, he and the other Beatles were too nervous about the new album to pay much attention to girls.

Their worries were for nothing. The album's release on June 1, 1967, caused an extraordinary sensation. The critics loved it, calling it "remarkable" and "pure poetry."

One wrote, "Over the last four years, Lennon and McCartney have developed into the greatest songwriting team of this century." *Time* magazine gushed that the album "represented a historic departure in the progress of music—any music." One thing was certain: *Sgt. Pepper's Lonely Hearts Club Band* was a runaway bestseller, topping the pace of all previous Beatles albums with a staggering 2.5 million copies sold in the first three months of its release.

A whole new type of Beatlemania broke out, not powered by screams and swoons as before, but rather by a kind of reverence in which every note the band played and word they sang was analyzed and dissected for greater meaning. Critics devoted columns and lectures to the Beatles' cultural significance. Some people called them "messengers from beyond rock 'n roll." And one famous philosopher, Timothy Leary, called them "evolutionary agents sent by God, endowed with mysterious powers to create a new human species."

But even in the midst of this very productive period, there were notes of discontent. Professionally, the Beatles felt the strain of a tight bond now entering its tenth year. They had been inseparable for the most part, shaping one another's attitudes toward life and dreams about the future. As boys, they had clung to one another—to the Beatles—for stability and even survival, but as men, they were looking beyond the band for their individual needs.

George found the "assembly-line process" of recording "a bit tiring and a bit boring." To him, the whole Sgt. Pepper's business had been a turnoff. "A lot of time it ended up with just Paul playing the piano and Ringo keeping the tempo, and we weren't allowed to play as a band so much," he complained, not unjustly. Certainly there was less for George to do on this album. Guitar parts seemed to have taken a backseat to technical fireworks. And most of the songs he proposed doing had been rejected by John and Paul.

Whatever restlessness George felt in the studio was compounded by John's self-loathing. The effects of LSD, along with a tired marriage, sunk John further and further into an emotional shell. "I was in a real big depression in *Pepper*," John recalled. "I was going through murder."

John and Cynthia Lennon, October 1967. © MIRRORPIX

In picture after picture taken throughout the months of recording *Sgt. Pepper's,* John looks miserable, achingly sad, his eyes as flat and lifeless as those of a poached fish. Food no longer interested him, probably a condition caused by the drugs. "It was becoming almost impossible to communicate with him," recalled Cynthia, John's wife. John was often spaced out and behaved much like a child.

There was a lot of discontent brewing among the Beatles. As in any family, they were beset by the kind of jealousy that erupts into fights. Nothing that serious—at the moment. But it was impossible to tell when it might blow up into something more critical.

In the meantime, the band had agreed to participate in the world's first satellite TV broadcast, linking thirty-one television networks around the globe. An estimated 300 million people could conceivably watch the same show simultaneously. It was designed to allow each of the participating countries a five-minute segment in which to feature material or an act that represented its culture. And, of course, what could be more British than the Beatles?

John had just finished writing "All You Need Is Love," which, according to George Martin, "seemed to fit with the overall concept of the program." As the broadcast drew near, however, the Beatles realized that performing it live, without a safety net, so to

Visiting with Maharishi Mahesh Yogi in 1967. © MIRRORPIX

speak, was risky. They'd become used to taking their time in the studio, overdubbing and correcting mistakes. Nothing was left to chance anymore. The Beatles hadn't performed live in almost a year. There was no telling how they would sound.

"By 7 PM [on the evening of the broadcast], the studio appeared to be in chaos," reported a friend. But despite all the turmoil, between miscues and mischief, the Beatles performed "All You Need Is Love" for the world without a hint of disorganization. They sat perched on stools placed directly in front of some guests, appearing as cool as only the Beatles could look under the circumstances. Their voices synched beautifully, perfectly, to a backing track. It sounded effortless, done in one take, much the way they'd fired off "Twist and Shout" four and a half years earlier: rock-steady and right on.

• • • • •

Now that that musical ordeal was over, the Beatles looked outside the studio for some personal peace and quiet. They all felt a little bit of emptiness in their souls, to say nothing of the fact that they had been through intense, nonstop craziness for the past four years. So on August 24, 1967, three of the Beatles (Ringo was visiting his wife, Maureen, in the

184

hospital, where she had just given birth to their second son) attended a lecture given by Maharishi Mahesh Yogi, an Indian spiritual leader whose message promoted love, peace, and eternal happiness.

The Maharishi was a spidery little man who dressed in a gauzy white robe and sat cross-legged on a deerskin mat strewn with flowers. He advised John, Paul, and George "to look within in order to find peace." And he suggested they learn how to meditate. By meditating, he said, they could reach a state of cosmic consciousness, which was blissful and beautiful. George, Paul, and John thought he made a lot of sense. They quickly explained the lecture to Ringo, who was always supportive of the others' whims, and on August 25, all four Beatles, along with their wives or girlfriends and several friends, left London for a campus in Wales, where they planned to take part in a weeklong retreat given by the Maharishi.

• • • • •

Brian Epstein remained behind to take care of business and host a dinner party at his country estate. For months, he had been grappling with personal problems, including severe depression, which had put him in a dark funk, and he looked forward to blowing off some steam without worrying about the Beatles. But as the weekend lingered on, he fell into an even darker mood, and after some guests cancelled their plans to attend his dinner, he drove back to London.

It must have been hard for him to get to sleep, so Brian took some pills—very powerful pills—to help him drift off. The next morning, when an assistant showed up, he was still in bed. After banging on Brian's locked bedroom door for a long time and getting no answer, she called a doctor, who broke down the door. Inside, everything was perfectly still, including Brian, who was lying on his side.

An hour later, one of Brian's assistants telephoned the retreat where the Beatles were staying and asked to speak to Paul. "I'm sorry," he said, "but I'm afraid I've got bad news. Brian has died."

185

George and his wife, Pattie, arrive at the memorial service for Brian Epstein, October 1967. © MIRRORPIX

The Beatles had known little or nothing about the state of Brian's health or the extent of his depression. Still, all evidence indicated that his death was accidental. He had taken too many pills for his body to absorb at one time. At a hastily arranged press conference, the Beatles appeared bewildered. "This is a terrible shock," Paul told the reporters who had gathered there. "I am terribly upset." In the "confusion and disbelief" that followed the phone call, there was only numbness.

What could they do? Who would they turn to for advice? For the moment, Paul recalled, the Beatles went to see the Maharishi. "Our friend is dead," they told him. "How do we handle this?" Because Hindu teaching dictates that mortals not focus on death but on the transcendence of the spirit—the soul's moving on to another plain—the Maharishi's advice about Brian was "to love him and let him go" so that his soul could continue its upward journey. "You have to grieve for him and love him, and now you send him on his way."

John told reporters that Brian was just passing into the next phase. "His spirit is still around and always will be," he said. But deep down, John remembered thinking, "We were in trouble then." John admitted feeling "scared" about the Beatles' ability to function, to remain together as a group without Brian's instinct and finesse. Indeed, as soon as the news of Brian's death struck home, John thought, "We've...had it."

Chapter 11

A few days after Brian's death, Paul rounded up the other Beatles for a meeting at his house. When they pulled up outside, Paul was already waiting for them at the front door with his sheepdog, Martha. "Let's go upstairs to the music room," he said. "There is something we should get to without delay."

Paul felt that the best remedy for their shock was to do something together, something musical. He had been tinkering with an idea for a new project taken from one of his childhood memories. During the late 1950s, neighborhoods had sponsored "mystery tours" in which kids boarded a bus whose destination was kept secret. "Everyone would spend time guessing where they were going, and this was part of the thrill," he remembered. What would happen if the Beatles gave this idea a new twist? he asked the others. How cool would it be to comb the English countryside in their own private bus, stopping spontaneously in villages and towns to film nutty sequences? They could stage little scenes and provide an original sound track. And they could make it up as they went along, so that the Beatles wouldn't have to learn lines to a script, which they hated. It was loaded with possibilities. Before long, he'd imagined it as a groovy mystery tour—no, a *magical* mystery tour—to echo the spirit of the times.

Even though John, George, and Ringo were skeptical, Paul was convincing, so much so that he and John immediately fired off a title song with the opening line *"Roll up! Roll up for the mystery tour."* Despite the lack of a plan, a crew, or even a basic script, Paul wanted to begin filming *Magical Mystery Tour* right away, that very week. It was crazy, but their

YEAH! **YEAH! YEAH!**

lives as Beatles had been crazy from the start. This was something they could pull off easily, and it would help take their minds off Brian's death. Besides, they already had a bunch of songs they could use. Paul had written "The Fool on the Hill," and John was working on something called "I Am the Walrus," which was cluttered with zany wordplay. It all came together fast—perhaps too fast. "Some of the sounds weren't very good," according to George Martin. "Some were brilliant, but some were bloody awful." The Beatles, however, were clearly pleased with the album.

Production began immediately on the *Magical Mystery Tour* film, which proceeded in a haphazard manner. Other than Paul, no one had given it much thought. "We literally made it up as we went," he recalled. There was no real cast to speak of. Faces were the important thing; the Beatles wanted *characters,* eccentrics who would look and perform in outrageous ways. There were a couple of midgets, thanks to John, who, according to Ringo, "would always want a midget or two around." There were fat actors, people who could twist their bodies into wild shapes, and a few friends. They located a sixty-two-seat bus, an old yellow job on which they painted a *Magical Mystery Tour* logo that Paul had designed, and took off for the West Country with their cast and crew aboard.

For the most part, the tour was a mess—five days of chaotic shooting in and around Surrey and Devon, with visits to the Cornish beaches on the Atlantic coast. "We would get off the bus: 'Let's stop here,' and go and do this and that," Ringo recalled. "Then we'd put music to it." Occasionally, it worked, but often they encountered technical and logistical problems that interfered with their plans. Besides, the tour was hardly magical or

Paul McCartney by the *Magical Mystery Tour* bus, September 1967. © Mirrorpix

Beatles Merchandise

In all fairness, the Beatles should have reaped a merchandising windfall. Fans clambered for any product that featured the boys' images: dolls, stationery, lockets, wigs, songbooks, T-shirts, photos, pins, calendars, sweaters, scrapbooks, games, and more. There was even Beatles bubble bath and Beatles wallpaper. In February 1964, the *Wall Street Journal* predicted that US teenagers alone would spend $50 million on Beatles paraphernalia.

Unfortunately for the Beatles, that side of their operation was "a major rip-off." "The reality is that the Beatles never saw a penny out of the merchandising," according to a lawyer who later helped untangle their business affairs. The deals Brian Epstein made for them were atrocious, just bad. "Tens of millions of dollars went down the drain because of the way the whole thing was mishandled."

even a mystery, since the bus was trailed everywhere by a convoy of twenty or so cars filled with press and fans who blocked roads and snarled traffic.

Eventually, the Beatles had enough footage to string together an hour's worth of film, but everyone involved with the project knew this wouldn't be one of their masterpieces. "If Brian had been alive, he would have pulled it into some kind of professional shape—or talked the Beatles out of it," said a colleague from their management firm. But without him, the Beatles went full speed ahead.

• • • • •

Meanwhile, back at NEMS, everyone was fighting to take over Brian's job. The Beatles weren't interested in a manager at the moment, Paul told them. After all this time, the Beatles were finally on their own, free to make every decision as they alone saw fit.

The first thing they did was to form a new company called Apple Music Ltd., so named because, Paul maintained, *Apple* was the first schoolbook word that children learned: A is for apple. Then they sat around trying to figure out exactly what their new company would do. "We're just going to do—*everything!*" John told his old friend Pete Shotton. "We'll have electronics, we'll have clothes, we'll have publishing, we'll have music. We're going to be talent spotters and have new talent." John was *very* excited about the Apple idea.

To kick things off, Apple opened a clothing company. The Beatles were delighted by the idea of having their own boutique full of groovy clothes. Early in 1967, they had purchased a cute little building on Baker Street, which they intended to use for their new business empire, hiring some friends to paint a mural on its ancient white brick facade. Citywide, the Apple Boutique mural was a huge conversation piece. London had never seen anything like it. People came from every district to get a closer look, clogging the sidewalk outside the shop, tying up traffic.

Inside, however, the shop was a mess, beginning with the clothes themselves. "The clothes looked more like fancy-dress costumes than anything one could wear day to day," wrote an observer. "Court jester crossed with harlequin crossed with Peter Pan, rainbow colors, zigzag hems, ballet tights and operatic coats for flower children." The clothes were pretty to look at but completely impractical.

Meanwhile, John and Paul began to fight for control. "Paul wanted dividers up," recalled Pete Shotton, who was hired to run the place. "Then John would come in and say, 'Why in the hell are we cutting people off from each other?' and he'd have the dividers ripped out." There was much bickering back and forth. Each of the two Beatles wanted to put his own stamp on the store; each was suspicious and jealous of the other's contributions.

The Apple Boutique finally opened on December 7, 1967, with a by-invitation-only gala. From the

For a brief period, the Apple Boutique wore a forty-foot psychedelic mural painted by the Fool before neighborhood shopkeepers demanded its removal, December 1967. © HULTON-DEUTSCH COLLECTION/CORBIS

193

outset, the store suffered severe losses. "No one knew where anything was," recalled a friend. "People were stealing things left and right." Another friend said, "It was disastrous from start to finish."

In the midst of this wreck, another disaster loomed. On December 15, Paul gathered the Beatles and their friends to watch the final cut of *Magical Mystery Tour.* It was a fifty-odd-minute crazy quilt of scenes that had been pasted together without the slightest regard for a story. "There was no plot," Paul admitted. According to Neil Aspinall, the band's road manager, who had traveled with the Beatles from their very first days on tour, "Nobody had the vaguest idea what it was about." George Martin, who watched in openmouthed horror, thought "it looked awful and it was a disaster." Even John described it for a journalist as "the most expensive home movie ever."

John with Cynthia, and George with Pattie at Heathrow Airport, off to India, February 1968. © MIRRORPIX

The Beatles had dropped roughly £40,000 of their own money on *Magical Mystery Tour* up to that point. And the critics hated it. "Appalling!" the *Daily Mail* said. "It was worse than terrible." A writer for the *Evening News* advised readers to take their pick from the words "rubbish, piffle, chaotic, flop, tasteless, nonsense, emptiness, and appalling."

One disaster for the Beatles was uncommon, but two coming right on top of each other—well, two disasters were unimaginable. The band had always been very careful about how they conducted business. There were never any slipups when Brian was alive. But now that the Beatles were in charge of their own destiny, things had gotten a bit derailed.

To get their lives back on track, the Beatles made plans in February 1968 to spend three months at the Maharishi's ashram, or retreat, in rural India, a setting of natural simplicity where they intended to study Transcendental Meditation. It was the answer to the Beatles' prayers. "We were finally getting away from everything," John recalled—the craziness, the drugs, the fame, the grind. John and George and their wives arrived first; Paul (with Jane Asher, who was still at his side) and Ringo (with Maureen) followed three days later, where they joined their friends and sixty other students who were absorbed in quiet, thoughtful meditation. There was also plenty of time for talking, reading, and lazing in the sun.

George had become an instant convert to TM. But John more than anyone threw himself wholeheartedly into the practice. "I was meditating about eight hours a day," he recalled. Cynthia, who admitted to being surprised by his discipline, said, "To John, nothing else mattered. He spent literally days in deep meditation." He and George threw themselves

What Is Transcendental Meditation?

The Maharishi Mahesh Yogi educated the Beatles about the benefits of Transcendental Meditation, or TM, which they embraced wholeheartedly in the early months of 1968.

An ancient eastern form of spiritual meditation, TM is the process by which a person contacts his inner reservoir of creativity, energy, and intelligence by looking within himself in order to find peace. For twenty minutes a day, he is supposed to sit comfortably with his eyes closed, allowing the mind and body to become deeply relaxed. At the most settled state of awareness, according to the Maharishi, the mind transcends all mental activity to experience the simplest forms of awareness, or Transcendental Consciousness. One's breathing becomes softer, the muscles relax, and more blood flows to the brain, all of which helps lessen stress and fatigue.

"It's all in the mind," John explained. "It strengthens understanding and makes people more relaxed. It's not just a fad or a gimmick, but the way to calm down tensions."

Paul called the experience "almost magical" and still advises his kids to practice TM whenever they are "stuck somewhere...or a bit disturbed." It helped, he said, to "face your dangers" so "you will see that they're not what you thought they were."

totally into the Maharishi's teachings, which led George to pursue a purer lifestyle and renounce LSD. Paul recalled that he was "looking for something to fill some kind of hole." He acknowledged feeling "a little bit of emptiness" in his soul, "a lack of spiritual fulfillment." Even Ringo, whose enthusiasm for India was much lower than his friends', said, "It was pretty exciting. We were in a very spiritual place." Here they were happy, relaxed, and above all found a peace of mind that had been missing in their lives. Only Paul seemed less than satisfied. "It was quite nice," he thought at the time. But more and more he had "trouble keeping [his] mind clear," he said, "because the minute you clear it, a thought comes in and says, 'What are we gonna do about our next record?'"

Paul couldn't let it rest, not even in India during afternoons sunbathing with the others on the banks of the Ganges River. There was always a guitar within reach, always paper nearby on which to scribble the beginning of a song. Paul wrote like mad in India—but truth be told, so did John. "Regardless of what I was supposed to be doing, I did write some of my best songs while I was there," he recalled. John and Paul began meeting in the afternoons in each other's rooms. In all, they completed nearly forty songs. John wrote "Julia," "The Continuing Story of Bungalow Bill," "Mean Mr. Mustard," "Jealous Guy," "Across the Universe," "Cry Baby Cry," "Polythene Pam," "Yer Blues," and "I'm So Tired," while Paul tackled "Rocky Raccoon," "Wild Honey Pie," "I Will," "Mother Nature's Son," and "Back in the U.S.S.R."

Often in the evenings, the Maharishi led his young followers on excursions to the nearest village, where local tailors sat cross-legged on mats operating ancient sewing machines. The Beatles had traditional Indian outfits made—loose-fitting, gauzy shirts and wide pajama bottoms, and saris for the women—and shopped for souvenirs. They explored open-air markets and found restaurants that served cold, perspiring beakers of "forbidden" wine.

On one occasion, everyone trooped down from the meditation center along a dusty jungle path, swinging lanterns in the fading twilight. For some reason Paul had brought his guitar, and as they descended through the steep overgrowth, he serenaded the party with bits of a new song he'd been working on. *"Desmond has a barrow in the marketplace...,"* he sang gaily over the thrash of footsteps. The song focused on a Yoruba phrase he'd picked up from Jimmy Scott, a conga player. "Every time we met," Paul recalled, "he'd say, 'Ob la di ob la da, life goes on, bra,'" and the expression had stuck in Paul's head.

By now Paul and John had written enough good songs for two or three albums. "We're not here to do the next album," George scolded Paul. "We're here to meditate." But an album was already taking shape in Paul's mind. He was very satisfied with the songs he'd written and thought several of John's—particularly "Across the Universe" and "Bungalow Bill"— were among his partner's "great songs."

For Ringo, the urge to see his two children became overpowering, and after two weeks he and Maureen decided they'd had enough of the ashram. Besides, Maureen was frightened of the fist-sized insects that flew through their

Ringo Starr and his wife, Maureen, on their way to the transcendental meditation center of the Maharishi Mahesh Yogi. © BETTMANN/CORBIS

room, and Ringo couldn't handle the spicy curries. For them, it was time to go home. The same with Paul and Jane. Paul was never as committed to meditation as John and George were, and after a month, he decided to leave as well. He was concerned that John and George "might never come back."

"John took meditation very seriously," Cynthia recalled. His approach to it brought with it a remarkable change; he seemed happier, certainly healthier. But Cynthia was beginning to suspect the Maharishi's power over John, that there was some sort of mind control being used to wrestle her husband away from his career. "He seemed very isolated and would spend days on end with the Maharishi, emerging bleary-eyed and not wanting to communicate with anyone. He was so deeply within himself through meditation that he separated himself from everything."

It didn't occur to Cynthia that John was struggling to separate himself from her. For the past few weeks, they'd hardly exchanged a word between them, even in private moments. Knowing that John hated confrontations with her, Cynthia chose to ignore the bad vibes. "Something had gone very wrong between John and me," she concluded. "It was as if a brick wall had gone up between us."

It wasn't a brick wall, but paper: a flurry of postcards sent by a woman John had met in London, an artist, who intrigued him. The postcards arrived in India almost every day. John rose early and stole away to collect them at the postal drop near the dining hall. The postcards were like catnip for him; he couldn't resist getting the next one to see what kind of cosmic mischief the woman had cooked up. "I am a cloud," she scrawled on one. "Watch for me in the sky." "I got so excited about her letters," John recalled, that he couldn't stop thinking about her.

It wasn't the Maharishi, but Yoko Ono who had taken control of John's mind.

• • • • •

John had met Yoko at an art gallery in London in November 1966. He had gone to see a wacky new exhibit called "Unfinished Paintings and Objects." The friend who took him there called it "a real happening," which turned out to be an understatement. John buried himself in the exhibit's catalogue, reading the nutty entries: *"...mirror to see your behind... sky T.V....eternal time clock...Painting to hammer a nail...Painting to let the light go through... Crying machine..."* "Is this stuff for real?" he wanted to know. The descriptions sounded like a put-on. Then one of the exhibits caught his eye, and he moved in for a closer look. On a shelf were several nails atop a Plexiglas stand, and next to that, an apple—it looked real as far as he could tell—with a little card that said APPLE. When he asked his friend for the price of the apple, he was told £200. "This is a joke, this is pretty funny," he thought.

Suddenly, the artist, a slip of a young Asian woman, was at his side. She had an amazing presence, John thought. There was something strange and exceptional about her. "Hey, man," his friend said, "allow me to introduce Yoko Ono."

She showed him another exhibit that he loved—a piece of plasterboard with a small sign inviting visitors to hammer a nail into its surface. "You can hammer a nail in for five shillings," she said. Grinning, John responded, "I'll give you an imaginary five shillings if you let me hammer in an imaginary nail." It was pure Lennon humor, and Yoko loved it.

Afterward, over the course of several months, she tried to get John's attention. And somewhere along the line, something piqued his interest in her. He underwrote one of her nutty projects. He liked that she refused to play by the rules. She was a true original—like him. In Yoko, he saw a kindred spirit. And she *excited* him. She was unlike any other woman he'd ever met. A real challenge.

John Lennon with Yoko Ono at the "You Are Here" art exhibition, 1968.
© MIRRORPIX

199

Now, returning to London from India, he was occupied by thoughts of Yoko Ono. For weeks, he continuously thought about her. His marriage difficulties sent John into a deep depression, during which he drank too much and took drugs. While Cynthia was away on a vacation in Greece, John finally fell in love with Yoko. "I can't bear to be apart from her," he told a friend. As far as John was concerned, that was the end of his marriage. "I'm going to go and live with Yoko, even if it means living in a tent with her."

$$\bullet \bullet \bullet \bullet \bullet$$

John Lennon's marital problems couldn't have come at a worse time for the Beatles. They had just opened their new business venture, Apple Music, and were struggling with a scheme that invited anyone with a good idea to write to them for money. The promise of money and the Beatles was too much for people to resist, whether they had talent or not. "Overnight, we were swamped with calls and kids who wandered in demanding an audition," recalled their office manager. "Everyone tried to get through the door in the next couple of weeks." George called it "madness" and described the outcome as "basically...chaos."

George hated the new company and considered it a "ridiculous" idea from the start. He resented that all the decisions were being made by John and especially Paul. There were bad feelings brewing among them for the first time in their career. The Beatles had always been a tight-knit fraternity—one for all and all for one. Cynthia Lennon called it "a marriage of four minds that were always in harmony." *Always* may be too strong a word, but on those occasions when it became necessary to close ranks, the Beatles formed an airtight bond; there was nothing and no one capable of splitting up the core group.

Now, however, little jealousies began to crop up, threatening the stability of the band. For the first several months of getting Apple up and running, Paul took complete control of the operation. Which only made things worse for John. "They could never agree on *anything*," recalled an assistant at Apple. "Ego started becoming more important than success. John automatically blackballed any of Paul's suggestions. Paul killed George's; George rejected

John's." Even their forthcoming recording sessions for a new album, drawn from the songs they'd written in India, produced a fresh strain. Each of the Beatles argued for their personal songs. "The Beatles were getting real tense with each other," acknowledged John.

Part of the tension stemmed from his relationship with Yoko Ono. It had thrown his life into complete upheaval. When they appeared in public together, even the adoring fans were outraged. Where was Cynthia? they wondered. Who was this other woman? The Beatles were days away from beginning work on an important new album, and suddenly John's personal problems, not music, had become the group's primary focus.

But there were bigger problems to come. Throughout the early recording sessions for the new album, Yoko Ono sat by John's side. "It was fairly shocking," recalled an engineer who worked in the studio. There was an unwritten rule that wives and girlfriends never came to the studio. The boys never allowed visitors to watch them work. *Never!* In Paul's view, the studio was sacred, the Beatles'

John and Yoko celebrate their impromptu marriage with the Rock of Gibraltar as a dramatic backdrop, March 20, 1969. © MIRRORPIX

By 1969, it had come to this: dispassion—along with Yoko Ono—in the recording studio.   © Mirrorpix

relationship to it like "four miners who go down the pit"—and "you don't need women down the pit, do you?" Now, suddenly, Yoko had landed in the thick of things. She "just moved in," according to George, who was not at all pleased. After that she was always at John's side.

The other Beatles pretended that nothing unusual was going on. Inside, however, they seethed. They cut one another tense glances, furious at the intrusion but unwilling to confront John. Worse, perhaps, Yoko refused to remain a spectator. From the very first session of the new album, Yoko made it clear that she intended to *participate,* grabbing John's mike during one take of a song and moaning. The other Beatles were very angry at John. By allowing Yoko Ono to interrupt their session, he had crossed the line. "We were all trying to be cool and not mention it," said Ringo, "but inside we were all feeling it and talking in corners."

They tried to overlook Yoko, but she made herself difficult to ignore. She was always in their faces, making decisions about what instruments to use. "Beatles do this..." "Beatles do that..." Every time she interrupted, it sent a chill through the studio. She even instructed George Martin to throw away certain takes of songs. Finally, during the second week of work, Paul gave John a piece of his mind. "I could hear them going at it in the hall," recalled a studio employee, "and it was terrifying. Paul was positively *livid,* accusing John of being reckless, childish, sabotaging the group." But the more Paul fumed, the less John responded.

Yoko only brought to the surface resentments that had been brewing among the Beatles for the past year. John couldn't stand the way Paul insisted on doing things a certain way— *his* way. The kind of music John wanted to play was being upstaged by the material Paul was writing—more pop oriented and less raw rock 'n roll. And Paul was tired of dealing with John's drug-taking and seeming boredom with the recording process.

In the interest of cooling off, Paul left for a business trip to Los Angeles, where he announced the opening of the Beatles' new label, Apple Records. While he was there, Paul arranged to see a woman he had first met at the *Sgt. Pepper's* launch party in London, American photographer Linda Eastman. "The moment Linda arrived that was *it,* as far as other girls were concerned," said a friend who accompanied Paul on the trip. What he liked best about Linda, Paul recalled, was her take-it-as-it-comes attitude toward life. It was a relief from the more formal structure of his relationship with Jane Asher, to whom he had become engaged. Although Paul suggested they'd be seeing more of each other, he made no promises to Linda.

Jane still loomed large in his life, if not in his heart. For the longest time, Paul had had a hard time keeping up with her. Jane's diary, which she lived by, was a clutter of fascinating appointments and social commitments. "Paul was clearly in awe of her," recalled a colleague. But if anything, Jane now had a hard time keeping up with him. Paul was an internationally

"Hey Jude"

In the midst of John's divorce, Paul drove out to Kenwood to see Cynthia and Julian Lennon. He thought it was tragic for the two of them to be cut off from the Beatles family and wanted to let them know he was still their friend.

The trip out took about an hour, during which Paul passed the time singing, improvising a lyric to serve as "a hopeful message for Julian": *"Hey, Jools—don't make it bad; take a sad song and make it better..."* Throughout his visit with Cynthia and Julian, the tune kept turning over in his head. By the time he returned home, he was ready to put on the finishing touches.

Paul tied the song up neatly in one sitting, changing Jools to Jude, after a character in the Broadway show *Oklahoma!* whose name had the right ring. In his enthusiasm, he rushed to play "Hey Jude" for John and Yoko, who had arrived at his house as it came together. The couple was silent and sullen, not so easily impressed, but John later acknowledged the song as "one of [Paul's] masterpieces."

known figure, sought after as much by strangely dressed freaks as he was by distinguished diplomats and intellectuals.

"Jane confided in me enough to say that Paul wanted her to become the little woman at home with the kiddies," Cynthia wrote in a memoir. But that wasn't the plan Jane had mapped out for herself. According to another friend, Jane had "clearly decided that she was setting her own terms on how she conducted her career." There were to be no cop-outs, no compromises, no backseats taken to pop stars.

As far as Paul was concerned, their relationship was drawing to an end. And he was still very upset by John's recent breakup with Cynthia.

A week or two after returning to London, Paul drove out to visit Cynthia and her young son, Julian. He wasn't certain how John would feel about that, but he decided it was the decent thing to do. The trip to their house took about an hour, during which Paul passed the time writing a lyric as "a hopeful message to Julian": *"Hey, Jools—don't make it bad; take a sad song and make it better..."* His voice glided over the tune, a beautiful melody that drew the listener below its gentle surface like a lullaby. Later, Paul tied the song up neatly in one sitting, changing Jools to Jude, which had the right ring to it. John eventually acknowledged the song as "one of Paul's masterpieces."

Even so, it did little to alleviate the Beatles' problems. The recording session for their new album became more splintered. "I remember having three studios operating at the same time," recalled George. "Paul was doing some overdubs in one. John was in another, and I was recording some horns in a third." With the focus running in every direction, friction was inevitable. Tempers flared whenever one of the Beatles didn't get his way or disapproved of one of the others' favorite songs. John made no secret

The Lennon estate, Kenwood, during remodeling. © Mɪʀʀᴏʀᴘɪx

of the fact that he was "hurt when Paul would knock something off without involving" the rest of the band. George felt ignored by John and Paul, who dismissed his songs as lightweights. Even on "While My Guitar Gently Weeps," one of George's best compositions, he sensed that John and Paul were merely going through the motions. "They weren't taking it seriously," he recalled.

All these incidents began to take a toll. Even in the midst of such creative accomplishment, the Beatles' rock-solid support structure was crumbling.

Chapter 12

When the Beatles finished recording for their new album, they decided on a revolutionary release: a double album. John, George, and Paul had written "so much material" in India that to do otherwise would have meant scrapping too many good songs. George Martin was dead set against a double album, as were Ringo and George, but there was an agreement among the Beatles that the complete set was "definitely rocking" and deserved to be heard. It also deserved a suitably rocking cover.

A famous artist suggested they call it something as utterly simple as *The Beatles* and package it in an all-white cover, with nothing more than a title pressed into the front. The Beatles loved that idea. The UK release of *The Beatles*—known forever afterward as the White Album—on November 22, 1968 (exactly five years after *With the Beatles* appeared), was regarded as an international event, certainly, as one newspaper referred to it, "the most important musical event of the year."

For the time being, the album's success overshadowed the band's personal difficulties, but the Beatles' nerves were frayed. No one liked the direction in which things were heading. They were disgusted with the situation at Apple, which was in disarray. John more than anyone was growing increasingly dissatisfied. As he saw it, the band was content to continue making more Beatles records, content to continue as the lovable lads from Liverpool, which didn't interest him. He no longer found the Beatles' music intriguing. Worse, perhaps, he thought the "togetherness had gone" and said, "There was no longer any spark." Their musical and personal issues demanded a break with the past. So he

George Harrison in 1969. © MIRRORPIX

decided that it was time for him to leave the band.

The others were rightfully shocked. Breaking up the Beatles had never crossed their minds. Paul recalled: "Our jaws dropped. No one quite knew what to say." He was determined to hold the group together, but there was no way John wanted to be involved in any more Beatles escapades. The group was over as far as he was concerned.

Eventually John agreed to "give it a couple of months" so that they could work out some kind of strategy and to keep an open mind about the group. Music might help them patch things up. So they began work on another album, with a film crew shooting footage of the recording sessions for a future television documentary. But by the second week of rehearsals, tensions were at an all-time high. Ringo and George were bored; John wasn't into it. Only Paul was charged up at the sessions, choosing the songs, directing the cameraman, working to fire up the other Beatles' enthusiasm. Now it was George's turn to let anger show, and during a tense session at which Paul badgered him about how to play a simple guitar solo, George finally snapped. What am I doing here? he wondered. He packed up his guitar, banging the case shut with sharp, angry blows. "That's it. I'm out of here." And he stomped out.

George did not return at all that day or the next. John suggested replacing him with Eric Clapton, but it was pointless for them to continue without him. Finally, he agreed to return, but only if the others would work on the new album in a studio they were building at Apple. With George Martin's help, they got the place into working condition and began to jam like mad. "The facilities at Apple were great," Ringo recalled. "It was so comfortable and it was ours, like home."

The Beatles immediately banged out "Get Back" and "The Two of Us." There seemed to be a renewed sense of teamwork in the friendlier setting. But as the week wore on, tempers collided anew. More than ever, according to George, Yoko was putting out "negative vibes." She acted resentful toward the other Beatles. She found the band to be "very childish." And John withdrew behind her, becoming increasingly nervous and apprehensive. The Beatles' sound was something he "didn't believe in" anymore. John quickly changed the atmosphere in the studio. Once again, the Beatles started banging heads. "They started picking on each other," according to John. "It was a very tense period," Paul recalled.

By the end of January 1969, working together on the project had become completely unmanageable. During a lunch at Apple, everyone sat around

The Beatles' #1 US Hit Singles

1. "Love Me Do"
2. "From Me to You"
3. "She Loves You"
4. "I Want to Hold Your Hand"
5. "Can't Buy Me Love"
6. "A Hard Day's Night"
7. "I Feel Fine"
8. "Eight Days a Week"
9. "Ticket to Ride"
10. "Help!"
11. "Yesterday"
12. "Day Tripper"
13. "We Can Work It Out"
14. "Paperback Writer"
15. "Yellow Submarine"
16. "Eleanor Rigby"
17. "Penny Lane"
18. "All You Need Is Love"
19. "Hello Goodbye"
20. "Lady Madonna"
21. "Hey Jude"
22. "Get Back"
23. "The Ballad of John and Yoko"
24. "Something"
25. "Come Together"
26. "Let It Be"
27. "The Long and Winding Road"

debating how and where to finish the film. In the course of the conversation, Ringo mentioned that there was a wonderful open roof above their offices that they intended to turn into a garden. "Oh, that's fantastic," John remembered saying. Everyone immediately went upstairs to have a look.

The roof, as it turned out, held the answer to their problems. The unanimous opinion: What a great idea it would be to play on the roof—play to the whole of the West End of London. The Beatles could give a concert from the comfort of their own building. Just head upstairs, plug in the instruments, and let 'er rip. Brilliant! "Nobody had ever done that," George recalled, "so it would be interesting to see what happened when we started playing up there."

The whole thing was to be very spontaneous, a secret. Not even the Apple staff was given advance warning. The next morning, a cold, cloud-streaked day, a crew set up the Beatles' equipment while the film crew staked out territory along the outer walls of Apple. Not since the live broadcast for "All You Need Is Love" had the Beatles felt as excited or more like a band.

Just before noon, the haze burned off, the clouds rolled back, and the sun broke through. Before the first song, a breathless version of "Get Back," had even ended, the music had attracted a small lunchtime crowd of onlookers. Word began to circulate that the Beatles, who hadn't entertained in England for more than three years, were playing in public. All around, neighbors rushed into the street or raced to their own roofs to see what all the racket was about.

Eventually, the police showed up and requested that the volume be lowered. The police were friendly but insistent: "Honestly,

The final concert on the rooftop of Apple Records, as the Beatles, with Billy Preston, perform together—joyously—for the last time, January 30, 1969. © Mirrorpix

the music has got to go down, or there's going to be some arrests," they said. But it was too late. The Beatles had already managed to play just enough material to cover a full performance.

"I'd like to say thanks on behalf of the group and ourselves," John said, mugging into the camera, "and I hope we passed the audition."

• • • • •

Though the Beatles had dodged questions about the bubble bursting ever since they first landed in America, they couldn't help but feel the pressure mounting toward the inevitable, ugly bang. By March 1969, John, Paul, George, and Ringo knew the end was near. Months of bickering had steadily dispirited them. To ease the tension, they each became involved in personal projects: John and Yoko finished production of an avant-garde film for TV; Paul worked with a singer named Mary Hopkin, for whom he produced a song called "Those Were the Days"; Ringo accepted a role in a movie called *The Magic Christian*; and George recorded a solo album, *Electronic Sounds*, at his home. They still existed as the Beatles, but they were unable to summon either the means to resolve their differences or the courage to go their separate ways.

No one was prepared when rumors of Paul's marriage to Linda Eastman

Paul and Linda on the day of their marriage, London, March 1969.
© Cummings Archives/Redferns

Beatles US Albums

July 22, 1963, *Introducing the Beatles*, Vee-Jay Records

January 20, 1964, *Meet the Beatles*, Capitol Records

April 10, 1964, *The Beatles Second Album*, Capitol Records

June 26, 1964, *A Hard Day's Night*, United Artists Records

July 20, 1964, *Something New*, Capitol Records

November 23, 1964, *The Beatles Story*, Capitol Records

December 15, 1964, *Beatles '65*, Capitol Records

March 22, 1965, *The Early Beatles*, Capitol Records

June 14, 1965, *Beatles VI*, Capitol Records

August 13, 1965, *Help!*, Capitol Records

December 6, 1965, *Rubber Soul*, Capitol Records

June 20, 1966, *Yesterday...And Today*, Capitol Records

August 8, 1966, *Revolver*, Capitol Records

June 2, 1967, *Sgt. Pepper's Lonely Hearts Club Band*, Capitol Records

November 27, 1967, *Magical Mystery Tour*, Capitol Records

November 25, 1968, *The Beatles (White Album)*, Apple Records

January 13, 1969, *Yellow Submarine*, Apple Records

October 1, 1969, *Abbey Road*, Apple Records

May 18, 1970, *Let It Be*, Apple Records

began circulating around London. Paul and Linda had been seeing a lot of each other, first in New York, where Linda lived, and later in London, where she had come to seal their relationship. John, Ringo, and George might have been surprised by the sudden announcement, but none of them was shocked that he hadn't been invited to attend. "We're not even on speaking terms," George said. Marrying off the "last bachelor among the Beatles" was big news, and even a cold, driving rainstorm couldn't keep the fans from staging a crazy mob scene. The wedding, on March 12, 1969, resembled a page torn from the Beatlemania scrapbook.

Right about the same time, there was a mass firing at the Apple offices. The Beatles had decided to cut back on their expenses, and they dismissed almost everyone, even people who had been with them since the beginning, in 1962. The Apple Boutique was shut down, as were their electronics, film, and publishing divisions. There was also an ongoing battle among them about who would handle their business affairs now that Brian Epstein was dead. Paul wanted his new father-in-law, Lee Eastman, a well-regarded music lawyer, to fill the post, while John, George, and Ringo were in favor of a tough-talking business manager named Allen Klein. Neither side was willing to give an inch to the other. "We had great arguments with Paul," Ringo remembered.

Meanwhile, John and Yoko launched one crazy project after another, such as a press conference in Vienna at which they lay inside a large white sack, singing and humming, to promote a process they called "total communication." They also staged bed-ins—weekends where they stayed in a hotel bed while being interviewed—to promote world peace (although most people assumed it was to promote Yoko Ono). For another project, Acorns for Peace, they sent envelopes containing two acorns to the head of state of every country in the world so they could plant trees instead of making bombs. John was having so much fun stirring up trouble and manipulating the press with Yoko that nothing, not even the Beatles' money and legal hassles, was important enough to distract him.

Somehow, Paul persuaded the others to return to Abbey Road, for old time's sake, to work on a new studio album. Paul phoned George Martin to inquire whether he'd be available, or even willing, to make another Beatles album. Considering the way the group was arguing, Martin assumed he'd worked his last with the boys. "Only if you let me produce it the way we used to," he told Paul. John also had to agree, he insisted, but Paul assured him their decision was unanimous.

John was actually psyched to record. He was brimming with material, real edgy stuff. He confessed to a reporter that songwriting was "something that gets in your blood" and forced him to put aside old conflicts. "I've got things going around in my head right now, and as soon as I leave here I'm going round to Paul's place and we'll sit down and start [to] work."

Throughout May and into July they blazed through most of the album's basic tracks. They began with George's masterpiece, "Something," which he'd written for his wife, Pattie. It was an intensely stirring romantic ballad that would challenge "Yesterday" and "Michelle" as one of the most recognizable songs the Beatles ever produced. John and Paul had always thought that George wasn't in their league when it came to writing songs, but that opinion changed with "Something." George had also written "Here Comes the Sun," which held its own against the Lennon and McCartney songs on the album.

The work went well in the studio, but Yoko became an intruder again, this time with an even stranger twist. She was pregnant and under strict orders from her doctor to remain in bed. So she had a department store deliver a double bed to the studio and instructed an electrician there to suspend a microphone above her head so she could furnish her comments to the band while they recorded "Come Together."

The sessions eventually dwindled into chaos. "People would be walking out, banging instruments down, not turning up on time and keeping the others waiting three or four hours, then blaming each other for not having rehearsed or not having played their bit right," recalled an engineer on the session. Even so, the music remained sharp and daring. The

Lennon in bed with Yoko Ono at the Hilton Hotel, Amsterdam, peace protest, March 1969. © MIRRORPIX

band worked intently through the summer of 1969. At the beginning of August, they decided, almost on the spur of the moment, to shoot a photograph for the album cover. After much debate, they agreed to "just go outside, take the photo there, call the album *Abbey Road,* and be done with it." And sometime after ten o'clock in the morning, they marched onto the street to shoot the now-famous cover photo: John in a white suit and tennis shoes at the head of the pack; Ringo in black tails just behind him; Paul, wearing

215

navy blue and an open-necked shirt, trailing in third place; and George in a blue-jean outfit, bringing up the rear. John, impatient as ever, urged the others forward. "Come on, hurry up now, keep in step," he muttered. At the last minute, Paul kicked off his sandals and rejoined the procession barefoot. It was done in six quick shots, but it became perhaps the most famous album cover photograph ever taken.

• • • • •

By late August, with the album almost finished, John again expressed his wish to leave the Beatles. He'd already formed another band with Eric Clapton so that they could play rock 'n roll at a concert in Canada. Finally, at a meeting in October with the other Beatles, John told them he was getting a divorce. "What do you mean?" asked Paul, to which John responded, "I mean the group is over. I'm leaving."

The others didn't really believe him. "*Everybody* had tried to leave" the band at one time or another, according to George, "so it was nothing new." But John believed "they knew it was for real." Moments afterward, John burst into another room downstairs at Apple and shouted, "That's it—it's all over!"

And in a way, as Ringo noted, it felt like "a relief." He "knew it was a good decision." The constant sniping and fighting among "the lads," as he called the Beatles, had disturbed Ringo's gentle soul. Still, it was difficult for Ringo, who worried about what he was going to do with the rest of his life. George, on the other hand, had no regrets. "I wanted out myself," he recalled. "I could see a much better time ahead being by myself, away from the band. It had ceased to be fun, and it was time to get out of it."

As for Paul, his entire world, "since I'd been seventeen," he acknowledged, had been wrapped up in the group. He had so much invested in it, emotionally and personally. He loved the music they made, loved the recognition and the fans. Privately, he held out hope that John would come around. But in the weeks that followed, Paul lapsed into a depression. Some days he really missed the band, the guys and their horseplay, but there were also times he despised them. "Anger, deep, deep, anger set in," he recalled. He felt cheated. "And justifiably so because I was being screwed by my mates."

The other Beatles had betrayed him, Paul concluded, abandoned the dream they had shared. There was nothing he could do to restore their enthusiasm. The others seemed determined to go their own ways. For a few weeks they avoided one another. Any business was left to the accountants and lawyers. But Paul found it impossible to separate himself from the Beatles. He tried everything to distract himself from the overwhelming loss, but nothing seemed to capture his interest. He couldn't even get himself out of bed in the morning. He felt inadequate, empty, convinced that "I'd outlived my usefulness." The Beatles had given his life meaning. He spent hours, days, weeks, trying to make sense of the breakup, lashing out at anyone who attempted to draw him out of his funk. Instead of

Paul Is Dead!

On Friday, October 10, 1969, a Detroit disc jockey named Russ Gibb went on the air at WKNR-FM and astonished his listeners with the news that Paul McCartney was dead. In fact, he had been dead for several years, Gibb insisted. How did he know this? Gibb had reached this incredible conclusion after reading a college student's essay claiming that clues were presented on the *Abbey Road* cover.

On the cover, Gibb argued, Ringo was dressed in an undertaker's outfit, while Paul walked behind him barefoot, in the manner of a corpse prepared for burial in Italy. In fact, the picture itself resembled a funeral procession. The license plate of the Volkswagen in the picture was another tip-off: it read 28 IF, suggesting that Paul would have been twenty-eight if he had lived. There was more. On the back cover photo of *Magical Mystery Tour*, Paul wore a black carnation, while John, George, and Ringo wore red ones. Meanwhile, Paul was dressed in black, the other Beatles in white.

Gibb's announcement touched off rumors that swept across the globe. Every radio station jumped on the story, sending hundreds of thousands of fans scrambling to scour their Beatles records for clues. If "Strawberry Fields Forever" was played at 45 rpm instead of 33 ⅓, some listeners claimed, John sang the words "I buried Paul." *Paul is dead* became a slogan as familiar as almost any tune on *Abbey Road*. Everyone was convinced, except for Paul, who was very much alive and considered it "a bloody nuisance." Tracked down by reporters at his home in Scotland, he insisted, "For the record, Paul is *not* dead."

writing music, he spent hours outside "just planting trees" or helping Linda renovate an old farmhouse they'd bought in Scotland.

It never occurred to Paul just how much he missed John. More than anyone else, John had been his friend for ten years, to say nothing of his collaborator, his sidekick, his shadow. Not only had they played music together, they'd hung out together, dreamed together, became famous together, grown up together. Paul continued to hold out hope that their separation was temporary, but as the weeks, then months ticked away, Paul realized it was finished. He was angry at the Beatles—but even angrier at John. Without John, Paul finally admitted, the Beatles were indeed a thing of the past. That did not mean their music wouldn't live on, but the band as they knew it was done.

Then, one day just after Christmas in 1969, Paul emerged from his funk. He had a four-track recorder installed in his house and, in an attempt to get it together, began doing the only thing he knew how to do: making a new record. Only this time, he was making it by himself.

The other three Beatles had already moved on to other projects that expressed their new independence. Ringo was making an album of standards with the assistance of George Martin, while George was producing records on Apple for other artists. John was another story altogether. By late fall, his and Yoko's life together had become a traveling carnival of put-ons and misbehavior. They made some avant-garde films, staged peace festivals, and released *The Wedding Album,* a box of mementos from their marriage ceremony along with a record that contained one whole side of John and Yoko screaming each other's names.

Paul couldn't take any more of it. They had all agreed not to announce the band's breakup, but in an interview in April 1970, Paul finally spilled the beans. The *Daily Mirror* headline shot around the world: PAUL LEAVES THE BEATLES. Newspapers everywhere quickly picked up the story. "Beatle Paul McCartney confirmed today that he has broken with the Beatles—but 'did not know' if it was temporary or permanent."

What did John have to say about this? A reporter called him the next afternoon. John was angry. He had no idea Paul was going public with the news.

For an instant, Paul's announcement brought everything to a standstill. A silence filled the void. The music fell silent. All the tension melted away. For the moment, the world as they knew it stopped spinning, seemed perfectly at peace. As the Beatles, they had been to the toppermost of the poppermost, as John used to joke. They had encountered the crowds, heard the screams, felt the love. *Seen the light.* In a brief and shining interval, they had lived a dream that no Liverpool lad could imagine—a magical, fabulous dream out of a fairy tale. An unforgettable dream. "It was wonderful and it's over," John said to all those waiting for a sign. "And so, dear friends, you'll just have to carry on. The Dream Is Over."

But the legend of the Beatles had only just begun.

The Beatles, 1967. © MICHAEL OCHS ARCHIVES/REDFERNS

ENDNOTE

Even after the Beatles' breakup, there would be the release of *Let It Be*, in all its overproduced splendor, and then one after another Beatles rereleases—red album collections, blue album collections, rock albums, movie albums, number ones, and studio tapes, all exposing not just old fans but new ones to the magic and the myth. Each of the Beatles, with varying degrees of success, would go on to solo careers, cheesy duets (Paul), and gray-haired all-star supergroups (Ringo and George). There would be huge stadiums of fans cheering Wings, Paul's post-Beatles group, and strollers in Manhattan's Central Park who would smile as John and Yoko passed by, as if one of the most normal things in the world was one of the Beatles acting, well, like anyone else. There would be the December night in 1980 when a deranged man walked up to John outside his home and shot him in the back, ending his life. There would be the night nineteen years later when an intruder broke into George's home and stabbed him, then the Tuesday in 2001 when George succumbed to cancer. Ringo's ex-wife, Maureen, died of cancer in 1996; Paul's "lovely Linda" died of cancer, too, in 1998. But not all was grim.

There would be babies born to Beatles and to Beatles fans, millions of people who lived their lives to a sound track crafted by four Scouse boys who had either grown up or passed along. And the story changed as the players aged. Paul was no longer Paul—he was Sir Paul, knighted by the queen in 1997. John was no longer John—he was Saint John, a role model to angry young rock 'n rollers everywhere. George was no longer a third wheel—he was George Harrison, an artist in his own right and a humanitarian who organized benefit concerts to feed the poor and change the world, *something* and then some. And Ringo—well, he was still Ringo. Always would be. Sure, he married a former movie star, and his son Zak became the drummer he feared he would, but otherwise, life remained full of simple pleasures. The sickly boy who had almost died so many times outlived two of his bandmates and many others in this story. Lives begun together ended apart, as happens everywhere, even in pop songs.

But the Beatles were no longer just boys who had played rock 'n roll. They had been mere teenagers when it all happened; when the band split, Paul was all of twenty-nine years old; John and Ringo, thirty; and George, twenty-seven. But on the radio, on vinyl and cassette and CD, they became not kids, not a band, not anything like anything else. They were the Beatles. A vastness of talent, of charm, of genius, incomprehensible, an ocean like the one the four boys had once looked out on, peering west from the hills of Liverpool. And from them, a flood of song and love and pain and beauty, a flood that cascaded out of the Cavern and Hamburg and London into the world, a flow that pushed aside what had come before and, in the end, nourished.

· · · · ·

Once, always, and forever: the Beatles.

DISCOGRAPHY

US SINGLES

"My Bonnie" / "The Saints." April 23, 1962. Decca 31382 (Tony Sheridan and the Beat Brothers)

"Please Please Me" / "Ask Me Why." February 25, 1963. Vee-Jay VJ 498

"From Me to You" / "Thank You Girl." May 27, 1963. Vee-Jay VJ 522

"She Loves You" / "I'll Get You." September 16, 1963. Swan 4152

"I Want to Hold Your Hand" / "I Saw Her Standing There." December 26, 1963. Capitol 5112

"Please Please Me" / "From Me to You." January 30, 1964. Vee-Jay VJ 581

"Twist and Shout" / "There's a Place." March 2, 1964. Tollie 9001

"Can't Buy Me Love" / "You Can't Do That." March 16, 1964. Capitol 5150

"Do You Want to Know a Secret" / "Thank You Girl." March 23, 1964. Vee-Jay VJ 587

"Love Me Do" / "P.S. I Love You." April 27, 1964. Tollie 9008

"Sie Liebt Dich" / "I'll Get You." May 21, 1964. Swan 4182

"A Hard Day's Night" / "I Should Have Known Better." July 13, 1964. Capitol 5222

"I'll Cry Instead" / "I'm Happy Just to Dance with You." July 20, 1964. Capitol 5234

"And I Love Her" / "If I Fell." July 20, 1964. Capitol 5235

"Matchbox" / "Slow Down." August 24, 1964. Capitol 5255

"I Feel Fine" / "She's a Woman." November 23, 1964. Capitol 5327

"Eight Days a Week" / "I Don't Want to Spoil the Party." February 15, 1965. Capitol 5371

"Ticket to Ride" / "Yes It Is." April 19, 1965. Capitol 5407

"Help!" / "I'm Down." July 19, 1965. Capitol 5476

"Yesterday" / "Act Naturally." September 13, 1965. Capitol 5498

"Day Tripper" / "We Can Work It Out." December 6, 1965. Capitol 5555

"Nowhere Man" / "What Goes On." February 21, 1966. Capitol 5587

"Paperback Writer" / "Rain." May 30, 1966. Capitol 5651

"Eleanor Rigby" / "Yellow Submarine." August 8, 1966. Capitol 5715

"Strawberry Fields Forever" / "Penny Lane." February 13, 1967. Capitol 5810

DISCOGRAPHY

"All You Need Is Love" / "Baby, You're a Rich Man." July 17, 1967. Capitol 5964

"Hello Goodbye" / "I Am the Walrus." November 27, 1967. Capitol 2056

"Lady Madonna" / "The Inner Light." March 18, 1968. Capitol 2138

"Hey Jude" / "Revolution." August 26, 1968. Apple 2276

"Get Back" / "Don't Let Me Down." May 5, 1968. Apple 2490

"The Ballad of John and Yoko" / "Old Brown Shoe." June 4, 1969. Apple 2531

"Something" / "Come Together." October 6, 1969. Apple 2654

"Let It Be" / "You Know My Name (Look Up the Number)." March 11, 1970. Apple 2764

"The Long and Winding Road" / "For You Blue." May 11, 1970. Apple 2832

US ALBUMS

Introducing the Beatles. July 22, 1963. Vee-Jay VJLP 1062 (mono), SR 1062 (stereo)

A: "I Saw Her Standing There" "Misery" "Anna (Go to Him)" "Chains" "Boys" "Love Me Do"

B: "P.S. I Love You" "Baby It's You" "Do You Want to Know a Secret" "A Taste of Honey" "There's a Place" "Twist and Shout"

Meet the Beatles. January 20, 1964. Capitol T-2047 (mono), ST-2047 (stereo)

A: "I Want to Hold Your Hand" "I Saw Her Standing There" "This Boy" "It Won't Be Long" "All I've Got to Do" "All My Loving"

B: "Don't Bother Me" "Little Child" "Till There Was You" "Hold Me Tight" "I Wanna Be Your Man" "Not a Second Time"

The Beatles Second Album. April 10, 1964. Capitol T-2080 (mono), ST-2080 (stereo)

A: "Roll Over Beethoven" "Thank You Girl" "You Really Got a Hold on Me" "Devil in Her Heart" "Money (That's What I Want)" "You Can't Do That"

B: "Long Tall Sally" "I Call Your Name" "Please Mr. Postman" "I'll Get You" "She Loves You"

A Hard Day's Night. June 26, 1964. United Artists UA 6366 (mono), UAS 6366 (stereo)

A: "A Hard Day's Night" "Tell Me Why" "I'll Cry Instead" "I'm Happy Just to Dance with You" (two instrumentals by George Martin & Orchestra)

B: "I Should Have Known Better" "If I Fell" "And I Love Her" "Can't Buy Me Love" (two instrumentals by George

Martin & Orchestra)

Something New. July 20, 1964. Capitol T-2108 (mono), ST-2108 (stereo)

A: "I'll Cry Instead" "Things We Said Today" "Any Time at All" "When I Get Home" "Slow Down" "Matchbox"

B: "Tell Me Why" "And I Love Her" "I'm Happy Just to Dance with You" "If I Fell" "Komm, Gib Mir Deine Hand"

The Beatles Story. November 23, 1964. Capitol TBO-2222 (mono), STBO-2222 (stereo)

A: Interviews, excerpts from "I Want to Hold Your Hand" "Slow Down" "This Boy"

B: Interviews, excerpts from "You Can't Do That" "If I Fell" "And I Love Her"

C: Interviews, excerpts from "A Hard Day's Night" "And I Love Her"

D: Interviews, excerpts from "Twist and Shout" "Things We Said Today" "I'm Happy Just to Dance with You" "Little Child" "Long Tall Sally" "She Loves You" "Boys"

Beatles '65. December 15, 1964. Capitol T-2228 (mono), ST-2228 (stereo)

A: "No Reply" "I'm a Loser" "Baby's in Black" "Rock and Roll Music" "I'll Follow the Sun" "Mr. Moonlight"

B: "Honey Don't" "I'll Be Back" "She's a Woman" "I Feel Fine" "Everybody's Trying to Be My Baby"

The Early Beatles. March 22, 1965. Capitol T-2309 (mono), ST-2309 (stereo)

A: "Love Me Do" "Twist and Shout" "Anna (Go to Him)" "Chains" "Boys" "Ask Me Why"

B: "Please Please Me" "P.S. I Love You" "Baby It's You" "A Taste of Honey" "Do You Want to Know a Secret"

Beatles VI. June 14, 1965. Capitol T-2358 (mono), ST-2358 (stereo)

A: "Kansas City" "Eight Days a Week" "You Like Me Too Much" "Bad Boy" "I Don't Want to Spoil the Party" "Words of Love"

B: "What You're Doing" "Yes It Is" "Dizzy Miss Lizzy" "Tell Me What You See" "Every Little Thing"

Help!. August 13, 1965. Capitol MAS-2386 (mono), SMAS-2386 (stereo)

A: "Help!" "The Night Before" "You've Got to Hide Your Love Away" "I Need You" (three instrumentals by George Martin & Orchestra)

B: "Another Girl" "Ticket to Ride" "You're Going to Lose That Girl" (three instrumentals by George Martin & Orchestra)

Rubber Soul. December 6, 1965. Capitol T-2442 (mono), ST-2442 (stereo)

A: "I've Just Seen a Face" "Norwegian Wood (This Bird Has Flown)" "You Won't See Me" "Think for Yourself" "The Word" "Michelle"

B: "It's Only Love" "Girl" "I'm Looking Through You" "In My Life" "Wait" "Run for Your Life"

Yesterday...And Today. June 20, 1966. Capitol T-2553 (mono), ST-2553 (stereo)

A: "Drive My Car" "I'm Only Sleeping" "Nowhere Man" "Dr. Robert" "Yesterday" "Act Naturally"

B: "And Your Bird Can Sing" "If I Needed Someone" "We Can Work It Out" "What Goes On?" "Day Tripper"

Revolver. August 8, 1966. Capitol T-2576 (mono), ST-2576 (stereo)

A: "Taxman" "Eleanor Rigby" "Love You To" "Here, There and Everywhere" "Yellow Submarine" "She Said, She Said"

B: "Good Day Sunshine" "For No One" "I Want to Tell You" "Got to Get You into My Life" "Tomorrow Never Knows"

Sgt. Pepper's Lonely Hearts Club Band. June 2, 1967. Capitol MAS-2653 (mono), SMAS-2653 (stereo)

A: "Sgt. Pepper's Lonely Hearts Club Band" "With a Little Help from My Friends" "Lucy in the Sky with Diamonds" "Getting Better" "Fixing a Hole" "She's Leaving Home" "Being for the Benefit of Mr. Kite!"

B: "Within You Without You" "When I'm Sixty-four" "Lovely Rita" "Good Morning, Good Morning" "Sgt. Pepper's Lonely Hearts Club Band (reprise)" "A Day in the Life"

Magical Mystery Tour. November 27, 1967. Capitol MAL-2835 (mono), SMAL-2835 (stereo)

A: "Magical Mystery Tour" "The Fool on the Hill" "Flying" "Blue Jay Way" "Your Mother Should Know" "I Am the Walrus"

B: "Hello Goodbye" "Strawberry Fields Forever" "Penny Lane" "Baby You're a Rich Man" "All You Need Is Love"

The Beatles (White Album). November 25, 1968. Apple SO-383 (stereo only)

A: "Back in the U.S.S.R." "Dear Prudence" "Glass Onion" "Ob-La-Di, Ob-La-Da" "Wild Honey Pie" "The Continuing Story of Bungalow Bill" "While My Guitar Gently Weeps" "Happiness Is a Warm Gun"

B: "Martha My Dear" "I'm So Tired" "Blackbird" "Piggies" "Rocky Raccoon" "Don't Pass Me By" "Why Don't We Do It in the Road" "I Will" "Julia"

C: "Birthday" "Yer Blues" "Mother Nature's Son" "Everybody's Got Something to Hide Except Me and My Monkey" "Sexy Sadie" "Helter Skelter" "Long, Long, Long"

D: "Revolution I" "Honey Pie" "Savoy Truffle" "Cry Baby Cry" "Revolution 9" "Good Night"

Yellow Submarine. January 13, 1969. Apple SW-153 (stereo only)

A: "Yellow Submarine" "Only a Northern Song" "All Together Now" "Hey Bulldog" "It's All Too Much" "All You Need Is Love"

B: Seven instrumentals by the George Martin Orchestra

Abbey Road. October 1, 1969. Apple SO-383 (stereo only)

A: "Come Together" "Something" "Maxwell's Silver Hammer" "Oh! Darling" "Octopus's Garden" "I Want You (She's So Heavy)"

B: "Here Comes the Sun" "Because" "You Never Give Me Your Money" "Sun King" "Mean Mr. Mustard" "Polythene Pam" "She Came in Through the Bathroom Window" "Golden Slumbers" "Carry That Weight" "The End" "Her Majesty"

Hey Jude. February 26, 1970. Apple SW-385 (stereo only)

A: "Can't Buy Me Love" "I Should Have Known Better" "Paperback Writer" "Rain" "Lady Madonna" "Revolution"

B: "Hey Jude" "Old Brown Shoe" "Don't Let Me Down" "The Ballad of John and Yoko"

Let It Be. May 18, 1970. Apple AR-34001 (stereo only)

A: "Two of Us" "I Dig a Pony" "Across the Universe" "I Me Mine" "Dig It" "Let It Be" "Maggie Mae"

B: "I've Got a Feeling" "One After 909" "The Long and Winding Road" "For You Blue" "Get Back"

SELECTED BIBLIOGRAPHY

Badman, Keith. *The Beatles: Off the Record.* London: Omnibus, 2000.

Baker, Glenn. *The Beatles Down Under: The 1964 Australia and New Zealand Tour.* Sydney: Glebe, Wild and Woolley, 1982.

Beatles, The. *The Beatles Anthology.* San Francisco: Chronicle, 2000.

Best, Pete, and Patrick Doncaster. *Beatle! The Pete Best Story.* London: Plexus, 1985.

Best, Pete, and Bill Harry. *The Best Years of the Beatles!* London: Headline, 1997.

Braun, Michael. *Love Me Do: The Beatles' Progress.* London: Penguin, 1964.

Brown, Peter, and Steven Gaines. *The Love You Make.* New York: McGraw-Hill, 1983.

Clayson, Alan. *George Harrison: The Quiet One.* London: Sidgwick & Jackson, 1989.

——. *Ringo Starr: Straight Man or Joker.* New York: Paragon, 1991.

Coleman, Ray. *Lennon.* New York: McGraw-Hill, 1984.

——. *McCartney: Yesterday and Today.* London: Boxtree, 1995.

Davies, Hunter. *The Beatles.* 2nd rev. ed. New York: Norton, 1996.

DiLello, Richard. *The Longest Cocktail Party.* New York: Playboy, 1972.

Epstein, Brian. *A Cellarful of Noise.* London: Souvenir Press, 1964.

Fawcett, Anthony. *John Lennon: One Day at a Time.* New York: Grove, 1976.

Flippo, Chet. *McCartney: The Biography.* London: Sidgwick & Jackson, 1988.

Freeman, Robert. *The Beatles in America.* London: Mirror Books, 1964.

Goldman, Albert. *The Lives of John Lennon.* New York: William Morrow, 1988.

Green, Jonathon. *All Dressed Up: The Sixties and the Counterculture.* London: Jonathan Cape, 1998.

——. *Days in the Life.* London: Heinemann, 1988.

Harrison, George, with Derek Taylor. *I, Me, Mine.* New York: Simon & Schuster, 1980.

Harry, Bill. *The Beatles Who's Who.* London: Aurum, 1982.

——. *The Encyclopedia of Beatles People.* London: Blandford, 1997.

Harry, Bill, ed. *Mersey Beat: The Beginnings of the Beatles.* London: Omnibus, 1977.

Hopkins, Jerry. *Yoko Ono.* New York: Macmillan, 1986.

Kozinn, Allan. *The Beatles.* London: Phaidon Press, 1995.

Leigh, Spencer. *Drummed Out! The Sacking of Pete Best.* London: Northdown, 1998.

Leigh, Spencer, and Peter Frame. *Let's Go Down the Cavern.* London: Hutchinson, 1984.

Lennon, Cynthia. *A Twist of Lennon.* London: Star, 1978.

Lennon, John. *In His Own Write.* London: Jonathan Cape, 1964.

——. *A Spaniard in the Works.* London: Jonathan Cape, 1965.

Lewisohn, Mark. *The Beatles: Recording Sessions.* New York: Harmony, 1988.

——. *The Complete Beatles Chronicle.* New York: Harmony, 1992.

MacDonald, Ian. *Revolution in the Head: The Beatles' Records and the Sixties.* London: Fourth Estate, 1994.

Martin, George. *All You Need Is Ears.* New York: St. Martin's, 1979.

——. *Summer of Love: The Making of Sgt. Pepper.* London: Macmillan, 1994.

McCabe, Peter, and Robert D. Schonfeld. *Apple to the Core: The Unmaking of the Beatles.* London, Brian & O'Keefe, 1972.

McCartney, Mike. *Thank U Very Much: Mike McCartney's Family Album.* London: Barker, 1981.

Miles, Barry. *Paul McCartney: Many Years from Now.* New York: Henry Holt, 1997.

Norman, Philip. *Shout!* New York: Simon & Schuster, 1981.

Pawlowski, Gareth. *How They Became the Beatles: A Definitive History of the Early Years, 1960–1964.* New York: E. P. Dutton, 1989.

Riley, Tim. *Tell Me Why: The Beatles; Album by Album, Song by Song.* New York: Knopf, 1988.

Rolling Stone, Editors of. *The Rolling Stone Interviews.* New York: Paperback Library, 1971.

Schaffner, Nicholas. *The British Invasion.* New York: McGraw-Hill, 1982.

Sheff, David, and Barry Golson, eds. *The Playboy Interviews with John Lennon and Yoko Ono.* New York: Playboy Press, 1981.

Shotton, Pete, and Nicholas Schaffner. *John Lennon in My Life.* New York: Stein and Day, 1983.

Spitz, Bob. *Dylan: A Biography.* New York: McGraw-Hill, 1989.

Taylor, Derek. *Fifty Years Adrift.* London: Genesis, 1984.

——. *It Was Twenty Years Ago Today.* New York: Bantam, 1987.

Wenner, Jann. *Lennon Remembers.* New York: Fawcett, 1977.

INDEX

Page numbers in *italics* refer to photos.

ACKNOWLEDGMENTS

The author would like to acknowledge a great debt to the literally hundreds of people who generously contributed their personal stories and memories to the amazing Beatles saga. From the Scousers and the Liverpudlians and the Hamburg gang, everyone at NEMS, the swingin' Londoners, my fellow New Yorkers, all the musicians and record company folks, and Beatles fans throughout the world, there was a graciousness extended to me that went beyond simple cooperation.

I would especially like to thank my friends Angie and Sandy D'Amato for providing the yeah-yeah-yeah, Mary Finnegan for her enormous heart, my parents for their enduring love, and my daughter, Lily, to whom this book is gratefully dedicated, for inspiring this version of the story.

There is a long list of people at Little, Brown whose support for the project, to say nothing of hard, imaginative work, gave it shape and focus: Megan Tingley, Amy Hsu, Sangeeta Mehta, Betsy Uhrig, and especially Alvina Ling, whose careful reading of the manuscript and editorial expertise assured a first-rate outcome. Let me also pay tribute to Michael Pietsch, Geoff Shandler, and Marlena Bittner, who laid the foundation and whose contributions resonate on every page. My sincere thanks to everyone, and to Alison Impey for her great design and a supercool cover.

Of course, I always rely on the sage advice and encouragement of my agent, Sloan Harris, to steer me through the channels. These last few years he has gone to extraordinary lengths to keep me rock steady and on course, and I will be forever grateful.

Last, I am indebted to the Beatles and their incredible music for inspiring me throughout the ten years I devoted to this story, and for putting a smile on my face every time I hear one of their songs. They are truly fab and gear and groovy for providing the soundtrack to my life.